Improving Learning in Later Life

With life expectancy increasing, there is growing emphasis on encouraging older people to continue learning. This comes as part of a strategy to allow them to remain healthy, independent and vitally engaged in society for as long as possible. All the same, policy-makers have barely begun to address the issues involved and the perspectives of these learners.

This book presents insightful research that will help shift the focus of debate onto the learning experiences of older people themselves. It offers a critical overview of the development of theoretical and philosophical approaches to later life learning that have developed over the last three decades, drawing on published work from the USA, the UK, Australia and other countries. It documents the individual experiences of older people through a variety of methods, including:

- focus group discussions;
- learning diaries kept by older people;
- questionnaires considering, among other issues, older people's definition of what learning is;
- interviews and commentary.

This material gives a sense of the breadth and diversity of older people's experiences, as well as the enormous range of learning activities, both informal and formal, in which they are engaged in retirement. In a climate of debate and change concerning the provision and funding of non-vocational learning opportunities for adults of any age, this study's findings will be of particular importance. It will appeal to researchers and students of education as well as those directly involved in the implementation of courses and classes involving older learners.

Alexandra Withnall is Associate Professor at the University of Warwick. She has previously worked at the University of Lancaster, Keele University and the National Institute of Adult Continuing Education. She is a past chair of the UK-based Association for Education and Ageing.

Improving Learning TLRP

Series Editor: Andrew Pollard, Director of the ESRC Teaching and Learning Programme

Improving Learning in College: Rethinking literacies across the curriculum
Roz Ivanic, Richard Edwards, David Barton, Marilyn Martin-Jones, Zoe Fowler, Buddug Hughes, Gregg Mannion, Kate Miller, Candice Satchwell and June Smith

Improving Working as Learning
Alan Felstead, Alison Fuller, Nick Jewson and Lorna Unwin

Improving Disabled Students' Learning
Mary Fuller

Improving Learning in Later Life
Alexandra Withnall

Improving Mathematics at Work: The need for techno-mathematical literacies (forthcoming)
Celia Hoyles, Richard Noss, Phillip Kent and Arthur Bakker

Improving Research through User Engagement (forthcoming)
Mark Rickinson, Anne Edwards and Judy Sebba

Improving the Context for Inclusion: How teachers and educational psychologists can use action research to work together to develop inclusion (forthcoming)
Andrew Howes, Sam Fox and Heddwen Davies

Improving What is Learned at University: An exploration of the social and organisational diversity of university education (forthcoming)
John Brennan

Improving Learning by Widening Participation in Higher Education (forthcoming)
Miriam E. David, Ann-Marie Bathmaker, Gill Crozier, Pauline Davis, Hubert Ertl, Alison Fuller, Geoff Hayward, Sue Heath, Chris Hockings, Gareth Parry, Diane Reay, Anne Vignoles and Julian Williams

Improving Learning in Later Life

Alexandra Withnall

Routledge
Taylor & Francis Group

LONDON AND NEW YORK

First published 2010
by Routledge
2 Park Square, Milton Park, Abingdon, Oxon, OX14 4RN

Simultaneously published in the USA and Canada
by Routledge
270 Madison Avenue, New York, NY 10016

Routledge is an imprint of the Taylor & Francis Group, an informa business

© 2010 Alexandra Withnall

Typeset in Charter ITC and Stone Sans by
Keystroke, 28 High Street, Tettenhall, Wolverhampton
Printed and bound in Great Britain by
CPI Antony Rowe, Chippenham, Wiltshire

British Library Cataloguing in Publication Data
A catalogue record for this book is available from the British Library

Library of Congress Cataloging in Publication Data
Withnall, A.
Improving learning in later life / Alexandra Withnall.
p. cm.
Includes bibliographical references and index.
1. Older people–Education. 2. Continuing education. I. Title.
LC5457.W58 2010
374–dc22
2009006829

ISBN 10: 0–415–46171–5 (hbk)
ISBN 10: 0–415–46172–3 (pbk)
ISBN 10: 0–203–87253–3 (ebk)

ISBN 13: 978–0–415–46171–9 (hbk)
ISBN 13: 978–0–415–46172–6 (pbk)
ISBN 13: 978–0–203–87253–6 (ebk)

Contents

Illustrations

Figures

Tables

Boxes

Series editor's preface

The *Improving Learning* series showcases findings from projects within ESRC's Teaching and Learning Research Programme (TLRP) – the UK's largest ever co-ordinated educational research initiative.

Books in the *Improving Learning* series are explicitly designed to support 'evidence-informed' decisions in educational practice and policy-making. In particular, they combine rigorous social and educational science with high awareness of the significance of the issues being researched.

Working closely with practitioners, organizations and agencies covering all educational sectors, the Programme has supported many of the UK's best researchers to work on the direct improvement of policy and practice to support learning. Over sixty projects have been supported, covering many issues across the lifecourse. We are proud to present the results of this work through books in the *Improving Learning* series.

Each book provides a concise, accessible and definitive *overview* of innovative findings from a TLRP investment. If more advanced information is required, the books may be used as a gateway to academic journals, monographs, websites etc. On the other hand, shorter summaries and *Research Briefings* on key findings are also available via the Programme's website at www.tlrp.org.

We hope that you will find the analysis and findings presented in this book are helpful to you in your work on improving outcomes for learners.

Andrew Pollard
Director, Teaching and Learning Research Programme
Institute of Education, University of London

Acknowledgements

Special thanks are due to the many people who helped to bring this project to fruition especially the many enthusiastic older learners and their friends who so willingly gave their time to participate in all stages of the research. Professor Andrew Pollard, Director of the ESRC Teaching and Learning Research Programme (TLRP), and colleagues within the TLRP encouraged me to look at the findings again with the benefit of hindsight and have been a constant source of intellectual stimulation and friendly support. Professor Alan Walker, Director of the ESRC Growing Older Programme, and other GO colleagues were instrumental in sustaining my belief that ageing can be a positive experience and that there is much to be learnt from older people themselves. Victoria Thompson was Research Fellow in the early stages of the project and conducted some of the focus groups as well as taking responsibility for the design and dispatch of the questionnaires. Steven Martin revisited the quantitative data and helped to extend the analysis; and I am indebted to Brenda Maddison for her patient and accurate transcription of the interview data. I would also like to express my thanks, as ever, to all good friends within the Association for Education and Ageing and especially to Lesley Hart and Joanna Walker who acted as advisers to the project and freely shared their considerable expertise as well as offering their invaluable professional judgement.

Finally, I would like to thank Taylor & Francis for permission to reuse material that originally appeared as 'Exploring influences on later life learning' in the *International Journal of Lifelong Education*, 25 (2006): 29–49. I am also grateful to Professors John Field and Mal Leicester, editors of *Lifelong Learning: Education Across the Lifespan*, London: Routledge Falmer (2000), for permission to reuse material from my chapter 'Reflections on lifelong learning and the Third Age' (pp. 289–99).

Part I

What is the issue?

Chapter 1

Lifelong learning
A new climate for older learners?

Introduction

This book is based on a research project, *Older People and Lifelong Learning: Choices and Experiences*, originally funded through the Economic and Social Research Council's *Growing Older: Extending Quality Life Programme* (GO), which ran from 1999 to 2004. In 2005, following approval from the Programme's Steering Group, the research became an associated project within the ESRC's *Teaching and Learning Research Programme* (TLRP), joining other projects that were concerned with aspects of lifelong learning. It was felt that the research findings would add a new dimension to the Programme and would have specific relevance to the TLRP crosscutting theme of *learners through the life course*. This resurrection of the project afforded an excellent opportunity to revisit the data and to reconsider some of the findings in the light of more recent developments in lifelong learning and the growing interest in active ageing worldwide as well as, hopefully, making a worthwhile contribution to the overall work of the TLRP.

The idea for the research originated in much earlier developments. Awareness of demographic trends and an emerging interest in aspects of education and learning in retirement among a small group of academics, practitioners and researchers in the early 1980s had led to a series of annual residential meetings at Keele University where participants began to identify and to examine what they saw as emerging issues in respect of making provision for these older learners. The result was the formation in November 1985 of the Association for Educational Gerontology (AEG), since renamed the Association for Education and Ageing (AEA). The Association launched an academic journal and instituted an Annual Conference as well as making links with others working in the same field both in the UK and overseas and with various older people's organizations. Yet in spite of a steady flow of papers and articles that addressed a range of theoretical and practical issues in relation to education in later life, there had never been any well funded research in the United Kingdom (UK) that tried to explore older people's experiences of education and, more particularly, of learning over the course of their lives, the factors that might affect whether they choose to learn in retirement and what role learning might play in their lives as they grow older. This study set out to address these issues in some depth using a range of different investigative methods including participation by a small group of older people themselves as interviewers of their peers. The research was carried out between 2000 and 2002 and contributed to the *Growing Older Programme*'s overall findings in respect of aspects of social support for older people. It also attracted some fleeting media attention, and coincided with strenuous efforts from the National Institute of Adult Continuing Education (NIACE) to draw attention to the growing importance of later life learning through its *Older and Bolder* national development programme that was originally launched on a small scale in 1995 and was very successful in promoting the cause of the older learner. In 2008 this work was subsumed into the work of the NIACE Equalities Team and it is now intended to explore some new approaches and directions.

At this point it is important to clarify which older people are under discussion. At the outset, we took a decision not to make age a criterion for participation in our research but rather to concentrate on those people who are 'post-work' in that they are no longer involved in the work force on a full-time basis and/or have relinquished major responsibilities for raising a family. However, this did not preclude people who may be in some kind of part-time employment or voluntary work or have some caring duties perhaps for grandchildren or indeed for a disabled spouse or other family member. In this way, we hoped to involve a wide range of older people with a variety of commitments and different lifestyles in order to illustrate the very varied ways in which older people live their lives.

With its incorporation into the TLRP, we now present the original research project findings in the context of today's ageing society in which increasing numbers of older people are seeking opportunities to learn in a variety of settings and where the aspirations of the so-called 'baby boomers' are beginning to command attention as successive cohorts reach their sixties. What is apparent is that we can no longer afford to be complacent in respect of older people and their sheer numbers. The fact that many of them will have received a better education than their parents in a time of comparative peace and prosperity and that they can look forward to a reasonably healthy old age means that they will approach retirement, itself a changing concept, with a range of different expectations, hopes and dreams. Here we seek to explore further some of the issues that emerged within the study and to offer some pointers for the road ahead in the light of current policy developments in lifelong learning and their implications.

Certainly, the idea of lifelong learning has a familiar and comfortable ring to it; put simply, it implies an all-inclusive 'cradle-to-grave' approach to learning that offers the promise and availability of something for everyone whatever their age or situation. Indeed, its popularity as a slogan is illustrated by the fact that 1996 was designated European Year of Lifelong

Learning. Since then, discourses of lifelong learning have moved beyond mere slogan status to occupy a major place in the policy agendas of supranational organizations such as the World Trade Organization (WTO), the World Health Organization (WHO), the Organization for Economic Co-operation and Development (OECD), UNESCO and the European Union (EU) and subsequently, in those of different countries across the world. This growing focus on lifelong learning has spawned a veritable explosion of policy documents, a range of academic papers and articles written from a variety of disciplinary perspectives together with a seemingly never-ending debate about its definition and purposes together with analysis of ever-changing policies and practices in various different countries. At the same time, emerging demographic trends have raised awareness of the ageing of populations across the globe and the many challenges this is already bringing in tandem with rapid social, economic and technological changes affecting all areas of life.

This chapter begins with a brief overview of some of the issues that have emerged from recent debates concerning the nature and purpose of lifelong learning. It goes on to discuss some demographic trends and to examine some current thinking about the dynamic processes of ageing, notably the promotion of the concept of active ageing. Finally, it considers the extent to which older people as we have defined them here have featured within the discourses and policies of lifelong learning. Does lifelong learning offer a new climate in which older learners might flourish? This provides the context for an introduction to the aims and processes of the research study that is the main focus of the book, taking into account the time and the context in which it was carried out.

Perspectives on lifelong learning

Although notions of lifelong *education* are not new, it is generally agreed that ideas about lifelong *learning* first gained credence in Europe in the early 1970s as an increasingly important topic in debates within a range of international organizations. Its origins might be traced to what came to be known as the Faure Report (UNESCO 1972), a document that Schuetze has since described as having 'formulated the philosophical-political concept of a humanistic, democratic and emancipatory system of learning opportunities for everybody, independent of class, race or financial means, and independent of the age of the learner' (Schuetze 2006: 290). From a range of critical perspectives, a variety of authors have since traced the historical development of the concept of lifelong learning from its origins in this social justice model through different phases to its re-emergence in the 1990s as the basis for a new international debate about the role of education and training in relation to the perceived need for economic competitiveness in the face of globalization; and the growth of its acceptance as a desirable policy goal among a range of international organizations, especially the European Union (e.g. Brine 2006; Dehmel 2006; Schuetze 2006; Tuschling and Engemann 2006; Pépin 2007; Slowey 2008). Other commentators have observed the ways in which policies have frequently been interpreted and implemented in different ways in different countries (e.g. Green 2002; Healy and Slowey 2006; Prokou 2008; Slowey 2008). Meanwhile, Schuetze (2006) argues cogently that, in the conceptualization and implementation of policies on lifelong learning, the debates that have ensued and the agendas of international organizations are highly influenced by national governments that make use of them to promote and legitimize their own political agendas.

In a perceptive analysis of some of the models of lifelong learning that have emerged over time, Schuetze (2007) argues that lifelong learning, although mainly an umbrella term, is based on three principles that represent a break with the traditional front-end model of education. By definition, lifelong learning is 'lifelong', but it can also be 'life-wide' and centred on 'learning' as opposed to the traditional focus on education and educational institutions. Lifelong learning basically assumes that everyone should continue to learn throughout their lives. Life-wide learning draws attention to the fact that organized learning occurs in many different ways and in a variety of settings outside educational institutions. This obviously raises questions about the nature of knowledge and skills, how they are acquired and how individual learning might be recognized and assessed. At the same time, underpinning this focus on learning is the individual learner's motivation, capacity and responsibility to engage with learning, all of which depend on a range of other factors within people's lives, an issue further pursued by other writers such as Deakin Crick and Wilson (2005) and Lambeir (2005). Current models of lifelong learning identified by Schuetze (2007) are briefly summarized in Box 1.1.

Box 1.1   Models of lifelong learning

- The original emancipatory or social justice model where lifelong learning is available for everyone in the interests of equality of opportunity within a democratic society – the 'cradle-to-grave' ideal.
- Lifelong learning as a system of learning for citizens of democratic countries that includes opportunities for embracing modern technology that will enable on-line and distance learning, although the onus is on individuals to take responsibility for seeking out and engaging with available learning opportunities.
- The human capital model where lifelong learning refers to continuous work-related training and skill development in order to comply with the needs of the economy and of employers for a well qualified

> and adaptable workforce within a changing labour market in order
> to ensure economic competitiveness. Once again, individual workers
> are responsible for their own educational and skill development in
> order to boost their employability.
>
> (Schuetze 2007: 9)

Although the human capital model is currently dominant in the educational policies of many countries, Schuetze and Casey (2006) earlier
observed that none of these models actually exists in a pure form and that
official policy discourses change over time. Certainly, within Europe, the
European Commission produced a Memorandum on Lifelong Learning (EC
2000) followed by a Council Resolution (EC 2002) together with a subsequent stream of Communications on the importance of lifelong learning, in
which adult learning that encompasses learning for personal, civic and
social purposes as well as for employment-related aims has most recently
featured as an important component. Noting that participation by adults in
lifelong learning varies widely across the Member States, the Commission
adopted a Communication on Adult Learning in 2006 commenting that
'lifelong learning has a key role to play in developing citizenship and com-
petence' (EC 2006). This was followed by an Action Plan in September
2007 in order to help strengthen what appears to be an increasingly
complex adult learning sector across Member States. In particular, the most
recent Lifelong Learning Programme 2007–2013 is designed to provide
practical support for the implementation of adult learning policies. In its
Grundtvig strand, it encompasses all types of learning and, for the first
time, seeks especially to fund activities that will address the challenge of
an ageing population across Europe (EC 2007).

Accordingly, NIACE (2007) has concluded that the role of lifelong
learning within the European Union is now seen as important not just to
ensure economic competitiveness in the global economy but to promote
social inclusion and cohesion within ageing societies that are increasingly
diverse; and 'to ensure the well-being of individuals and communities who
are seeking to achieve their potential' (NIACE 2007: 5). Yet in respect of
the UK, NIACE has also commented that 'too often, public policy lurches on
a continuum between red-blooded utilitarianism and all-embracing, if
utopian, permissiveness' (NIACE 2007: 5).

Meanwhile, Aspin and Chapman (2007) talk about the 'vain quest for
definitions' of lifelong learning (2007: 20) that they regard as probably
inconclusive and ultimately self-defeating. They argue for the adoption of
a different approach.

> a more comprehensive analysis of all the various dimensions and
> features of the nature, aims and processes of policies for 'realizing a

lifelong learning approach to learning for all' will have to be tackled, and a more wide-ranging set of justifications addressing the differences in those aims and purposes more clearly articulated and provided.

(Aspin and Chapman 2007: 34)

Their point is that this more pragmatic approach will allow all the different desirable elements of lifelong learning currently advocated within Europe – economic progress, personal development and fulfilment and social inclusiveness – to cross-fertilize through the provision of a range of different initiatives. Yet as Edwards *et al.* (2002) have shown, a range of other writers has consistently questioned both the desirability and achievability of the various stated policy goals of lifelong learning. They critique the underlying assumption that the state has the ability to understand and interpret change and to devise appropriate policy responses and mechanisms. They further argue persuasively that any lifelong learning policy cannot achieve its aims because of this lack of understanding of change together with a failure to comprehend the diverse range of learning practices among people and the assumption that learning is cumulative rather than, as they see it, reflexive.

Whilst much of the debate on lifelong learning has obviously been concerned with aspects of policy analysis and implementation, Edward *et al.*'s subsequent argument that we need a theory of lifelong learning that 'entails the development of reflexive practices within learning relationships as they are manifested within different aspects of people's lives' (2002: 533) has its origins in earlier debates. For example, over a decade ago, Usher *et al.* (1997) were already questioning the prevailing 'cradle-to-grave' conceptualization of lifelong learning that nevertheless very obviously privileged vocational education and training in both policy and practice. Adopting a postmodern stance, they suggested that learning might be more readily located in social and cultural developments such as the growth of consumerism and in a range of social practices. More recently, Usher and Edwards (2007) have continued their exploration of how different social practices in which people engage become 'signed' as learning. They question how, if learning is lifelong and life-wide, it differs from other social practices and how such practices are given meaning as learning, why that occurs and what the consequences might be.

Over the years, there has been a range of other debates around the official discourses of lifelong learning such as the role of social capital (e.g. Kilpatrick *et al.* 2003). In a further development Leathwood and Francis (2006) have offered a far-reaching analysis of lifelong learning from a critical feminist perspective arguing for a more egalitarian and emancipatory approach that would make the gendered, classed and racialized nature of lifelong learning policies more open to scrutiny. Burke and Jackson (2007) take this approach further, drawing on both feminist and post-structuralist insights to argue forcibly for a reconceptualization of lifelong learning in ways that would support what they also term 'critical and reflexive communal and social learning' (2007: 215) although they argue that reflexivity can be a problematic concept. They also acknowledge how demographic trends are implicated in what they see as gendered constructions of lifelong learning within the UK. Overall, perhaps their main contribution to the debate is to draw attention to the need to open up what they call 'spaces of resistances, subversions and new possibilities' (2007: 201) in respect of lifelong learning, a development in which the reader is invited to participate.

These various approaches have served to challenge the modernist stance of many official policies on lifelong learning that tend to rest on assumptions of certainty, truth and rationality. To some extent, they have been important in drawing attention to the fragmented nature of different societies, to the impact of diversity in the population and to the potential of groups identified as having been previously oppressed and marginalized. Yet it is surprising that, until recently, older people had scarcely featured in the debate. Accordingly, at this point we turn to a consideration of the other issue raised at the beginning of the chapter: demographic trends and the implications of the ageing of the population for the development of lifelong learning policies and approaches to analysing them.

Growing older: active ageing?

The ageing of the world's population is well documented. In 2008, the United States Census Bureau estimated that 18 per cent of people across the globe were over the age of 50 with females outliving males in every decade, the biggest gap being between men and women aged 80-plus (US Census Bureau International Database 2008). In the UK, recent statistics show that 16 per cent of the population are already aged 65 or over, a growth of 31 per cent between 1971 and mid-2006. If pensionable age (currently 65 for men and 60 for women but due to change in 2010) is taken as the baseline, then the percentage is 18.7 per cent (Office for National Statistics 2007). During the same period, the population under 16 years old declined by 19 per cent. It is also worth noting that the largest percentage increase in the year to mid-2006 was at ages 85 and over, with 1.2 million people now in this age group, including nine thousand centenarians. It is predicted that this rise in the older population will continue at least for the first half of the twenty-first century as the greater numbers of people born just after the Second World War (the so-called 'baby boomers') enter their sixties and move into retirement (Office for National Statistics 2007). However, the statistics quoted do not include people aged 50 to 60 (women) or 50 to 65 (men). In other arenas, 50 appears to have become the preferred age for the designation of 'older adult', which implies that there are even greater numbers of 'older' people in the population than statistics choose to show, especially if we include those who are post-work.

In relation to statistics and the somewhat alarmist picture they often paint, Katz (1996) has already argued that the mere presentation of such statistics means little when taken in isolation from issues of economic status and social policy. The bald presentation of statistical facts also disguises the diversity and heterogeneity of older populations in different countries and stands to be accused of perpetuating a 'them and us' mentality. In this way, it becomes all too easy to see older people as a different species from the rest of the population rather than acknowledging that everyone is ageing and that old age will increasingly be experienced by greater numbers of people. Older people's issues are relevant to every generation and should be everyone's concern.

The emergence of the Third Age

What can be said is that, as the numbers and thus the visibility of older people in the population have increased, the processes of ageing have attracted attention from a range of disciplinary interests. For our purposes, it is the transformation of the institution of retirement as the result of trends in labour force participation that is of interest. During the 1990s, both Walker (1996) and Phillipson (1998) explored the ways in which the meaning of retirement was changing. Phillipson argued that it had evolved from a period of stability in the 1950s and 1960s when it was associated with (mainly male) exit from the workforce and entry into a state old age pension scheme to a phase of considerable instability and accompanying loss of identity for people who are post-work. He pointed out that the age at which people were actually leaving the workforce had come to depend on a variety of factors such as redundancy, voluntary severance, health problems, caring duties or the possibilities offered by flexible retirement policies or self-employment. With current plans to raise the state pension age to 65 for women in 2010 and to 68 for both sexes in 2020 in the UK, the situation is set to change again. Nevertheless, increased longevity still means that the post-work period is likely to be lengthy and, as Blaikie (1999) has shown, this change in the balance of life stages has considerable social and cultural outcomes. Yet this issue is only just beginning to attract the kind of attention it deserves. We shall return to a discussion of retirement later.

One of the identifiable outcomes has been the tendency among commentators to talk of a division of the later life period into the 'young old' and the 'old old'. A more recent popular designation has been that of the 'Third Age' of active leisure and personal fulfilment and the 'Fourth Age' of descent into dependence, senility and death. In defining the Third Age as the crown of life, Laslett (1989) foresaw that it would become a considerable and increasing part of everyone's experience and that therefore society needed to adjust to the cultural requirements of members of this group, themselves perceived as the cultural trustees of the future. It is important to note that he saw the Third Age not necessarily as an easily defined period of time but rather as a *status* that would be achieved through personal choice. For most people retirement and freedom from the constraints of work would be the period when this was easiest to operationalize, although planning should have begun well in advance. However, Laslett recognized that the uncertainties surrounding the arrival of the Fourth Age posed some difficulties for his theory of the Third Age although he argued that there are some Third Age activities that can still be pursued even in the face of physical decline.

In examining the imagery of the Third Age, Blaikie (1999) points out how Third Agers have been encouraged to develop a new kind of retirement lifestyle in which the emphasis has shifted from issues of sickness and decline towards the maintenance of good health and a sense of liberation. This change of emphasis, he shows, lies with the emergence of consumer culture, particularly as businesses become aware of demographic trends and more sensitized to the mature market. Indeed, as he notes, even a cursory reading of any of the current range of magazines aimed at older people shows them to be underpinned by a strongly upbeat philosophy. The wide variety of positive images of later life they contain and the opportunities they promote were certainly not available to previous generations of older people whose expectations would have been quite different. However, as Blaikie also points out, issues of gender, class, race and ethnicity and geographical location require far more exploration in understanding how the experience of living in the Third Age is actually structured by socio-economic and other factors such as health status largely outside individual control. Meanwhile, Gilleard and Higgs have examined the Third Age as 'a cultural field whose boundaries escape the confines of any specific community of interest' (2005: 3). Whilst acknowledging the inequalities of gender and ethnicity, they choose to focus on class, cohort and community as a way of analysing how older people engage with and give meaning to the Third Age.

Policy responses to ageing

In spite of this positive emphasis in developed countries and the growth of academic interest in later life, the potential impact of the ageing of populations is now a source of concern in many countries of the world to the extent that several organizations operating on a global scale now have large-scale programmes in place to identify and to begin to address some of the pressing issues. Indeed, the aim of the designation of 1999 as the United Nations International Year of Older People having as its theme 'a society for all ages' was to promote the United Nations Principles for Older People adopted by the UN General Assembly in 1991, i.e. independence, participation, care, self-fulfilment and dignity. Older people's 'access to appropriate education and training programmes' was specifically mentioned under the principle of 'independence'. The International Year was generally considered to have been very valuable in helping to raise awareness, to advance research and policy action on ageing across the world and to focus attention on multigenerational relationships.

A more recent important development was the WHO's contribution in the shape of a proposed policy framework to the Second United Nations World Assembly on Ageing held in Madrid in 2002. Defining older people as those aged 60-plus, this framework was based on the WHO's adoption of 'active ageing' as a way of enhancing quality of life as people grow older. Advocating a life course approach to active ageing, the policy framework has three pillars – health, participation and security – with a major component of participation being lifelong learning that will ensure older people are supported by educational policies and programmes for both men and women as they grow older.

The Second UN World Assembly on Ageing itself resulted in the publication of the Madrid International Plan of Action on Ageing (United Nations Programme on Ageing 2006), which had a number of central themes. One of these explicitly noted the need for the provision of opportunities for individual development, self-fulfilment and well-being throughout life as well as in later life, through, for example, access to lifelong learning and participation in the community. This document also acknowledged that older people are not a homogeneous group, an issue often overlooked in the rush to address ageing issues in different parts of the world. Unfortunately, it appears that national capacity to implement the Madrid Plan is very variable across the globe, depending largely on the extent to which countries have the necessary infrastructure and ability to promote ageing issues as well as the possibilities of promoting regional partnerships between major stakeholders (United Nations General Assembly 2006).

Walker (2002) has shown that, although the slogan 'active ageing' is relatively new within Europe, it has a longer history dating back to the early 1960s when it was considered to be the key to 'successful' ageing, especially in the USA. However, Walker considers that it has potentially more than slogan status. He outlines the key principles that he believes should be embodied within any notion of active ageing, suggesting that it should be a preventative concept that involves all age groups across the whole of the life course and including all older people even if they are frail and dependent; active ageing must be seen as intergenerational. It would embody both rights and obligations, possibly the most contentious aspect, and must be both 'participative and empowering' (2002: 125) as well as respecting diversity. To achieve these aims, it would be necessary to base the concept of active ageing on the idea of a partnership between the citizen and society. Walker goes on to give examples of how this might be operationalized across the life cycle throughout Europe. In later life older people would have expanded opportunities and the freedom to choose between different types of activities although it seems that their level of participation would be dependent on what they could afford. Nevertheless, if frailty intervened, the goal should still be participation and autonomy.

Walker's argument is an attractive one but it may be no more than seductive rhetoric disguising a utopian view of how active ageing might, in theory, be interpreted and operationalized. Suffice it to say here that, in recent years, the reality is that the concept of active ageing has gained unquestioned popularity as a strategy for ensuring that as people work longer and retire later, they are encouraged to take responsibility for engagement with their immediate communities, for their own health and well-being and, in general, for being as self-reliant as possible. The necessity to continue learning throughout life is frequently seen as an integral part of any such strategy; accordingly, the rhetoric of active ageing has entered the debate on later life learning as discussed further in the next chapter.

Withnall (2008) has investigated the issue further by examining a selection of recent national policy statements on both lifelong learning and on ageing populations across the four countries of the UK, the Republic of Ireland, the USA, Australia and New Zealand. She notes that, in spite of good intentions, it is arguably a difficult task to fully understand the complexities facing different countries and to compare their levels of success in addressing the wide range of questions that have emerged to date in respect of their ageing populations. Even if they operate within broadly similar political, economic and social systems, the dynamics of policy-making may vary between countries, as does the degree of urgency in addressing the challenges that the nature of the ageing of the population may produce. It may also be the case that entrenched beliefs about older people as a problem may be harder to overcome in some countries than in others (United Nations General Assembly 2006). Yet, of the countries investigated, Withnall notes that only the Republic of Ireland has no definitive strategy for its older population, possibly because the proportion of older people there is still comparatively low although the Irish government is well aware of the potential impact of future population growth.

Where the importance of learning in later life has been acknowledged, the basis on which provision can be justified varies among the countries studied; but there is evidence that the UN Principles for Older People and the WHO's advocacy of active ageing have been particularly influential in encouraging countries to recognize that learning for older people, albeit for different purposes, is vital where there is an ageing population. Any rationale for learning in later life was found to be located in a mixture of some or all of the statements listed in Box 1.2. This was accompanied in almost all cases by an acknowledgement that older people must be valued as a resource for society and that age discrimination in any form should not be tolerated. However, there was sometimes an underlying assumption that, in return, older people should have an obligation to take advantage of available education and training opportunities or to remain active in other ways, a view advocated by Walker (2002).

Box 1.2   Rationale for older people's participation in lifelong learning

- As a way of maintaining and developing skills and competences, including IT, with increased economic and social benefits to older people themselves, their families, the community and the economy.
- As a way of remaining independent for as long as possible.
- As part of health promotion that will enable older people to live longer free from chronic illness and disability.
- As a dimension of social inclusion and participation in civic life.
- As a way of understanding and respecting diversity.
- As a way of promoting empowerment, choice and personal growth.

(Withnall 2008: 24)

Withnall remarks on the language used in some of the strategy documents, which she describes as 'well intentioned but ultimately empty rhetoric' (2008: 25). She also comments that such an enthusiastic emphasis on active ageing tends to ignore the larger structural issues that may affect older people's ability to be active – for example, access to healthcare, transport issues, poor housing, lack of information and educational guidance as well as individual situations that may change over time. She argues for the need for educational policies in respect of older people to be developed in tandem with attention to other issues that affect their lives since educational policy-makers cannot bring about change on their own in view of the wide range of outcomes to which it is proposed learning should contribute.

There is also a danger that 'keeping active' becomes a moral imperative. Certainly, there are many more 'passive' activities many older people enjoy that they might quite legitimately describe as learning; other older people may prefer a quieter, more reflective life in which they develop their own self-directed activities based on hobbies or interests. The need to unpack ideas of 'activity' in relation to late life has been discussed by Katz, who warns of the potential dangers of 'management by activity' (2000). The important point seems to be that older people should be afforded choice whatever their personal circumstances and preferences. However, as already seen, to reconstruct later life simply as a period of lifestyle choice and opportunity is to ignore the realities of the socio-economic structure and the broader consequences that affect many older people's lives. Certainly choice is not a straightforward issue, as economists have demonstrated.

Lifelong learning revisited: the aims and processes of the study in context

This brief overview of perspectives on lifelong learning and on policy responses to demographic trends suggests that any recognition of the importance of older people being enabled to go on learning post-work is rarely to be found within any realistic vision of lifelong learning. Few of the lifelong learning policies developed in different countries have hitherto had much to say about learning in later life in view of the current emphasis on the importance of vocational education and training and, in the UK, on remedying the perceived skills deficit within the working population, although there is at least an acknowledgement within the latest EU Grundtvig Programme (Withnall 2008). However, whilst different policy statements relating to the ageing of populations and the promotion of the concept of active ageing appear to offer a more hopeful picture, it has been shown that the likelihood of implementation of the various strategies proposed by different organizations and governments is dependent on a very diverse range of factors and that progress is uneven or non-existent.

Sadly, it appears that the situation has worsened since the idea for our study was first conceived in the late 1990s. At that time, Edwards (1997) had already shown how various different analyses had been skilfully welded together by different interests to produce a powerful discourse that had been particularly influential in stressing the need for lifelong learning policies to support economic competitiveness in spite of the lip service then paid to the notion of learning as 'cradle-to-grave'. Tight's (1998) close analysis of three major policy reports related to the development of lifelong learning in the UK at that time had also revealed a strong priority accorded to vocational education and training in spite of some general rhetoric about the non-economic, personal and social benefits that lifelong learning could bring. Certainly, the Green Paper *The Learning Age* that followed and that drew partially on these reports emphasized the importance of developing a learning culture that would encourage personal independence, creativity and innovation and spoke of the family and community as sites for learning although it gave no place to a coherent philosophy of lifelong learning (DfEE 1998). The subsequent White Paper *Learning to Succeed*, which set out the government's new framework for post-16 learning, acknowledged that 'older people, for example, benefit greatly from learning' (DfEE 1999: 55) but devoted only a short paragraph to them, stressing little more than the role they could play as grandparents in family learning. It appeared that older people who were post-work were generally to be excluded from debate. It was apparent that they were generally marginalized in educational policy circles by the continuing emphasis on economic imperatives alongside other emerging concerns about the financial support of an ageing population that, although of considerable importance, tended to conceptualize later life as problematic. These debates have not gone away in the intervening years.

Part of the problem may have been that, whilst there was some welcome recognition that older people might benefit from educational activity, there was little understanding of older learners and the kinds of learning in which they might be involved. Until very recently, even the developing area of enquiry that has come to be known as educational gerontology, although subject to redefinition over the years and in different national contexts, tended to focus on the perspective of providers of educational opportunities rather than on older learners themselves. Where learning was mentioned at all in relation to later life, there was little attempt to distinguish between formally provided educational opportunities and the formal and informal learning which older people might undertake, much of which might be unrecognized even by older people themselves. Indeed, it was not at all clear how 'learning' was interpreted by different groups of older people and there was very little research that investigated whether older people had preferred and trusted ways of learning that continued to influence them post-work.

We concluded that a new formulation that seemed to offer a way forward would be to focus on *learning* as discussed above, rather than on *education* in later life. We began from the proposition that a conceptualization of lifelong learning that paid only lip service to the post-work population was inadequate. Learning itself might be more readily located in social and cultural developments such as the growth of consumerism and in a range of social practices (Usher *et al.*, 1997). Indeed, Gilleard (1996) was already developing his argument that contemporary consumer culture had played a part in helping older people to shape their identities at a time when the meaning of growing old was subject to revision at a time of rapid change. In a sense, it appeared that learning opportunities for adults generally were themselves becoming part of the consumer culture, offering the promise of access to a particular lifestyle and often marketed with enjoyment as the main aim.

Educators of adults have long argued, of course, that learning does not have to take part in formal settings and to be structured by formal providers as represented by the concept of learning that is 'life-wide'. The success of the mutual aid model University of the Third Age as it has developed in Britain and in Australia (discussed in the next chapter), and indeed other similar informal and self-help endeavours, has shown that some older people do not necessarily wish to buy into a lifestyle but that other factors may be important in assisting them to shape a post-work identity. This might include undertaking learning to better their opportunities; or it might mean, for example, a conscious decision to embark on an individual learning project or resume a neglected interest or simply to seek out like-minded people. Learning may also be unanticipated or imposed; the plethora of publications describing the early stages of widowhood and the subsequent necessity of learning to cope with a range of unfamiliar tasks is a case in point. Alternatively, learning in later life may consist of the kind of individual reflection and life review that takes place in an unstructured and spasmodic way but which may lead to greater self-understanding and individual insight: what would probably be recognized as 'wisdom'.

This suggested the need for a better understanding of what learning means in the context of older people's lives, whether they do make choices about learning in both formal and informal contexts in an uncertain world and the basis on which they might do so. It was also important to assess what outcomes learning might have for those in later life. However, the very heterogeneity of the post-work population and the sheer diversity of experience of different groups of older people further suggested that we needed to find a way to understand the influence of different events and beliefs over the life course and to problematize their experiences as learners. A life course approach assumes that learning activity in later life and the forms it might take at different times will be influenced by a complex interplay of individual characteristics and by a variety of individual and collective experiences over a lifetime as well as by both past and current opportunities, experiences and situational constraints. It offered the possibility of developing a distinctive perspective on the mechanisms influencing older people to continue or to take up learning post-work or indeed, not to do so. It also provided a way of investigating the relationship between learning undertaken in formal or in informal contexts and would encourage reflection on that learning which is unintentional or unanticipated.

The definitive questions that needed to be asked were wide-ranging. For example, how do older people themselves define and understand learning post-work? What value do they place on learning (and education)? What are the contexts and discourses over the life course that have shaped their perceptions? How have they constructed and developed ideas and attitudes to learning and to education? What outcomes do formal or informal and other types of learning have for older people in the context of their own lives and how are these outcomes experienced and described? These were the questions that underpinned the study in the hope that they might also help us to focus on a broader issue: what are the implications for theory and for social and educational policies in general in respect of a stronger emphasis on learning in later life? The life course approach has gained in popularity in recent years since it provides a way of examining how lives change within the wider changing social structure (Jamieson 2002). However, it is a dynamic approach and is therefore not without its methodological problems since it needs to incorporate a holistic picture of an individual's life covering a range of aspects, as Blaikie (1999) has observed. Jarvis (1994) had already attempted to address some of these issues, and Jamieson et al. (1998), whilst espousing a provider perspective, used the life course approach in a small-scale empirical study of a group of older people attending a residential summer school. Although offering a basic framework for understanding education in the context of retirement, they admitted that their study focused on a small and atypical group of older people. We considered that what was needed was a conceptual model of the pathways to, and forms of involvement in, post-work learning activity and an understanding of the consequences in order to inform debate and to help build a firmer foundation for future policy and practice.

These were the issues that informed the study. In obtaining empirical data, however, it also became apparent that this kind of thinking required a new research paradigm that would make ageing itself the focus of the debate and which would establish collaborative and non-exploitative research relationships by positioning older people themselves at the centre of the research process as well as developing what might be termed a reflexive approach at all stages. We argued that it might then be possible to move towards a new and more inclusive approach to lifelong learning that would have relevance for a society experiencing demographic and other kinds of change at an unprecedented rate.

The methods adopted in the study are discussed in detail in the Appendix. They are noted briefly in Box 1.3.

Box 1.3   Methods used

- Ten focus group discussions with groups of older people currently participating in a formally organized course or class in order to explore their perceptions of their involvement in education and learning activities over the life course and the influences on it. The findings would be used to develop a preliminary model of these influences in relation to later life learning.

- In order to test the validity of the model, a postal questionnaire to one hundred other older people, fifty of whom would be involved in formally organized learning activities and fifty not so involved but who might have been undertaking other types of learning or recognized that they were learning informally. Information would also be elicited about experiences of learning in later life.

- Fifty semi-structured interviews (twenty-five from each group) exploring the meaning ascribed to learning activities in greater depth.

- Analysis of twenty-five learning 'logs' or diaries to be kept over a period of two months.

- Construction of a new model incorporating the findings from the interviews and the logs.

Conclusion

In spite of the changing official rhetoric of lifelong learning and the enthusiastic promotion of the concept of active ageing within different strategy documents, older people still tend to be largely ignored in educational policy circles. At the time of our study, comparatively little was known about their experiences of education and of learning over the course of their lives, the factors that might affect whether they choose to learn post-work and what role learning plays in their lives as they grow older. In outlining our approach, we stressed the need to develop a research strategy that would place ageing at the centre of the debate and that would draw on a variety of different investigative techniques including inviting older people themselves to participate in the study, and to incorporate a reflexive approach at all stages. However, prior to discussing the findings of the study, it is essential to put the research into context. In the next chapter, we will briefly examine the development of various perspectives on education and learning in later life.

Chapter 2

Why learning in later life?

Introduction

In spite of some positive rhetoric we have seen that policies and discourses of lifelong learning have, until very recently, generally failed to consider the wider potential of making educational opportunities available to the post-work population. Neither have they acknowledged the aspirations of older people themselves as they embark on their post-work lives. The aim of this chapter therefore is to highlight the issues through a critical overview of the development of key approaches to learning in later life – what has come to be broadly known as educational gerontology – over the last three decades drawing on material from a range of countries. What ideas have been promulgated and where have they come from? We shall trace the emergence and development of educational gerontology, and conclude with a comment on the comparative absence from the debate of the voices of older learners themselves.

Social gerontology and educational gerontology

An initial step is to consider the nature of gerontology itself, a term that is broadly used to describe the study of ageing that, in view of the complexity of the human organism, inevitably requires the involvement of a whole range of disciplines that can include the social sciences and humanities as well as the physical and biological sciences. It is generally, but not always, considered separately from geriatrics, a branch of medicine that addresses the clinical care of older people. For our purposes, it is the emergence of social gerontology, broadly concerned with ageing in a social context, that is of particular interest even though attempts to delineate the territory are fraught with difficulty.

Jamieson (2002) in a succinct overview of the historical development of theory and practice in social gerontology seeks instead to establish what binds a complex and multifaceted 'field', if that is the appropriate term, together. She notes that, since social gerontology is itself a multi-disciplinary endeavour, what she terms the partial theories, concepts, frameworks and perspectives that have been developed are necessarily drawn from other disciplines. A further issue is that if social gerontology is concerned with ageing it is perhaps surprising that, until comparatively recently, the focus of much gerontological research has been on understanding aspects of later life itself rather than with the processes of growing up and growing older. Certainly, although there is increasing interest in developing a life course perspective and in exploring the nature of an ageing society (Phillipson 1998), there is still considerable emphasis on seeking to understand how older people live out their daily lives, the opportunities available to them, the constraints they face and, in the light of these, the nature of the choices they make. However, the range of methods that might be used to explore different aspects of later life has expanded considerably over the years, demonstrated by the wide variety of investigative strategies reported by researchers, including the emergence of interest in involving older people themselves in the processes of research (Barnes and Taylor 2007).

How is educational gerontology related to these developments and what are its origins? As Findsen reminds us, educational gerontology has had 'a spotty history' (2005: 1). It has been an area of debate that has engaged a range of both academics and practitioners in exploring various different aspects of the nature of later life learning, initially in the USA but latterly across the globe. Although it is generally accepted that the term first appeared in 1970 as the title of a doctoral programme at the University of Michigan, a definition can be traced to the work of the American writer Peterson who saw it as 'a field of study and practice that has recently developed at the interface of adult education and social gerontology' (Peterson 1976: 62). He suggested that educational gerontology consists of three distinct but interrelated aspects. The first of these is concerned with educational opportunities for older people; the second relates to education for the public about older people and ageing; and the third is the issue of education for professionals and paraprofessionals working with older people. Phillipson (1983) noted that, in 1982, the Institute of Gerontology at the University of Michigan was running an educational summer seminar programme for those working with older people with an emphasis on a positive approach to ageing and the potential of education to help build on their existing skills and abilities. There was also discussion around the emerging shape of, and future prospects for, the development of educational gerontology. Yet it is notable that, two years after Peterson published his definition, Sherron and Lumsden had referred to educational gerontology as 'a dynamic, fast-growing new branch of social gerontology' (1978: xi) rather than making any connection to the education of adults. Later, they went on to discuss the extent to which it had become legitimized as an academically respectable branch of social gerontology (Sherron and Lumsden 1990), a view that has persisted in some quarters. For example, Engelbrecht, writing more recently in an Australian context, adopts

Peterson's original definition of educational gerontology but confounds the debate by describing it as 'originating from the discipline of social gerontology' (2006: 56).

Yet this was not the case elsewhere. The situation in Europe was rather different, as Glendenning has shown in his overview of developments in what he terms 'the education for older adults "movement"' (2000a: 1). Probably the most significant advance at that time was the formation in Toulouse in 1973 of the University of the Third Age, its defining characteristic being that of older people studying specially designed courses on a university campus, taught by university faculty and with government funding. Although other Universities of the Third Age (U3A) developed differently in different parts of France, the rapid spread of the movement across a range of other European countries and beyond is well documented (Swindell and Thompson 1995). In particular, the British self-help model of U3A, formed in Cambridge in 1981 and embracing the medieval idea of a university as a community of scholars 'joined together in the selfless pursuit of knowledge and truth for its own sake' (Midwinter 1984: 4), might be seen as one of the major educational innovations in the education of adults over the last three decades. However, it borrowed only its title from the French innovation; in other respects, it was very different. One of its founders described its *modus operandi* as follows.

> In the University of the Third Age (U3A), as it began in Britain . . . every member is expected to learn, and, if he or she is in a position to do so, to teach as well. There is therefore no division between teacher and taught: there are no staff and students, only members . . . They can choose their own subjects, their own teachers, their own methods of learning.
>
> (Laslett 1989: 172)

In addition, various other examples of innovative approaches to the development of educational activities for older people could be discerned at that time (Johnston and Phillipson 1983). From 1986, the British government-funded Unit for the Development of Adult Continuing Education (UDACE) operating under the auspices of NIACE briefly dabbled with exploring educational opportunities for older adults, resulting in the publication of a handbook to guide local authorities and other interested agencies in making suitable provision (Harrison 1988). Overall, a stronger vision of the part that educational and other agencies and institutions, including the mass media, could play in stimulating new and more democratic forms of educational provision for, by and with older people was slowly beginning to emerge.

Accordingly, educational gerontology at this time was tethered mainly in the adult education stable; there was little attempt to connect with social gerontology and, indeed, few academic gerontologists made any attempt to engage with educational issues, at least in the UK. Meanwhile, the formation of the Association for Educational Gerontology (later renamed the Association for Education and Ageing or AEA) in 1985 meant that the definitions were again subject to debate. Whilst Peterson's concept of educational gerontology and some of his later writing had been influential in informing early thinking in the UK, it was felt to be inadequate by Glendenning (1985), who can be credited with raising awareness of the potential of educational gerontology in the UK and beyond. He proposed that, in British terms and arising from British practice at that time, it would be better to make a distinction at the outset between educational gerontology and gerontological education. In particular, he stressed the development from the 1970s onwards of senior self-help educational initiatives, particularly those that had emerged within the British model of U3A. He further argued that the nature of this self-help phenomenon required its own theory and methodology.

In fact, Glendenning went on to examine the relationship between educational and social gerontology in more detail at a later date, returning to a discussion of his earlier distinction between educational gerontology and gerontological education. Now he expanded his thinking about educational gerontology to suggest a comprehensive framework for learning in the later years that would incorporate instructional gerontology; senior adult education; self-help instructional gerontology; and self-help senior adult education. Gerontological education (the teaching of gerontology) would include aspects of social gerontology incorporating adult education in respect of curriculum development, tutor training and associated issues; advocacy and professional gerontology; and gerontology education covering post-professional and post-qualifying training and in-service training as well as the role and needs of carers. He briefly returned to a discussion of the close relationship between educational and social gerontology, concluding that adult education is essential to both; but he rejected any idea of educational gerontology as a 'branch' of social gerontology (Glendenning 2000b). Indeed, he was probably ahead of his time in his comprehensive vision. Some of the issues he raised are only now coming to be seen as important in thinking about older people's role in society.

At the same time, Lemieux and Sanchez Martinez (2000) entered the debate through their own discussion of whether educational gerontology should be seen as part of gerontology or as a component of education. Having considered previous debates about the multidisciplinary nature of gerontology and reviewed the work of both Peterson and Glendenning, they proposed the concept of 'gerontagogy' as a new 'hybrid' interdisciplinary science in education that would be concerned with all components of teaching older people and their learning in the same way as the concept of 'andragogy' was developed to refer to issues around learning in earlier phases of adult life as a process model with pedagogy seen as more of a content model (Knowles *et al.* 1984). However, there was a lengthy and extensive academic debate during the 1970s and 1980s about the assumptions underlying ideas of andragogy and their validity, the general conclusion being that we need to exercise considerable caution in making any claim for the distinctiveness of andragogy as a theory of adult learning or model of teaching (Smith 1996, 1999). If this is the case, then any attempt to impose an additional ideological category seems doomed to failure. It can also be argued that we should acknowledge that 'the aims and purposes of education and learning for older people should, in fact, be no different from those of people of any age group' (Percy 1990: 236). We shall return to this point later.

Although it will be seen that other debates have come to the fore in recent years, especially in view of the kinds of policy developments in lifelong learning already discussed, in practice the possibility of closer working relationships between social gerontologists and academics and practitioners with interests in aspects of later life education and learning, more broadly conceived, has slowly begun to emerge. This may be partly due to growing acknowledgement of demographic trends throughout the world and the subsequent expansion in opportunities for debate concerning the nature of growing old in different societies. In particular, the expanding number of national and international conferences addressing ageing issues now attracts participants from a wider range of countries, disciplinary backgrounds and interests.

Perspectives on education and learning in later life

A particular concern over the last three decades or so among those with an interest in education for older people has been to justify the post-work population as worthy of inclusion in educational policy decisions. Although the number of attempts that have been made to address the fundamental philosophical issues involved and to engage in theory building has been somewhat limited, we now turn to an overview of the different perspectives that have emerged.

Activity theory

A brief review by Withnall and Percy (1994) suggested that many of the early arguments were located within a functionalist paradigm and derived mainly from activity theory and from sociological theories of role change (Havighurst 1963). The emphasis in approaches that utilize role theory, as in activity theory, is that older people must deal with role loss and adjustment to role change in retirement. Activity theory sees later life as a time of potential individual growth and renewed social relationships; life satisfaction derives from social interaction and active participation so that the post-work period can be a positive, creative and busy time. In this way, the purpose of educational activity in later life is to provide solutions to the problem of how to achieve 'successful' ageing through the preservation of a positive, healthy and active lifestyle or through adaptation to a socially acceptable role. There is an implicit assumption that education can contribute to this process by assuring good health, well-being and personal satisfaction in later life. Activity theory opens the door for educators of adults to develop what they see as appropriate interventions and legitimates their claims to be able to offer older people choice and opportunity for keeping their brains active and healthy, for personal fulfilment and for self-development, although the meanings that might be ascribed to these terms have rarely been explored in any depth. Indeed, older people's very limited mention in the UK government's original plans for the development of its lifelong learning strategy was primarily based on the grounds that learning can have positive health outcomes (DfEE 1999).

The assumption was explored further in a DfEE-commissioned study of the motivation to learn in later life and its impact. Although the researchers noted the very considerable methodological difficulties of assessing the impact of learning on health status, they argued that their findings suggested that learning can contribute to health and social interaction and help to enrich an older person's life, usually as part of a wider set of activities (Dench and Regan 2000). Other evidence is patchy, and some researchers tend to generalize about older people as though they were a homogeneous group. However, as we have seen, this line of thinking has informed a number of recent strategy documents on ageing, albeit with a broader vision of what active ageing might entail. In the UK, it has found expression in the government's various responses to the challenges of an ageing population, discussed more fully in Chapter 6.

Any further debate has therefore tended to be framed in terms of older people's participation (or non-participation) in formally organized activities (Withnall and Percy 1994; Findsen 2005) together with discussion of appropriate provision for older people as one of a range of identified target groups often labelled as 'disadvantaged' (e.g. McGivney 1990) or 'socially excluded'. Over the last decade in the UK, it has found practical expression in NIACE's *Older and Bolder* national development programme. Initially, this initiative utilized a mixture of statistical and anecdotal evidence to make a strong case for increasing public investment in learning provision for older people (Carlton and Soulsby 1999). Later on, the *Older and Bolder* team worked tirelessly with government departments, various older people's organizations and individuals 'to encourage the idea that education has a role to play in developing and maintaining a good quality of life for older people' (Soulsby 2005). To this end, the programme concerned itself with issues such as financial literacy, information, advice and guidance and issues of cultural diversity in later life. In an evaluation of the first ten years of its activity, some of those who had been involved in its work in an advisory capacity identified a long list of very commendable practical achievements and considerable success in raising awareness across a range of government departments and other agencies as to how access to educational opportunities might improve the quality of later life. However, a few respondents commented on the lack of a strong research base and any rigorous evidence to underpin the programme's work (Withnall 2007a).

Some neurological research suggests that mental training in later life can boost intellectual power, assist in maintaining mental function and help to reverse memory decline (Kotulak 1997; Mehrotra 2003), as does current interest in the potential of 'brain training' games and activities and in the role of meaning and emotion in adult learning (Wolf 2006). Cohen (2005) also argues convincingly for the creative potential of the older mind. However, little of this work has yet impacted on educators working with older adults in a systematic way, and they have tended to proceed on the basis of a range of generally unproven assumptions.

It can be argued that activity theory may be far too limited to capture the complexity of older people's engagement in social activities and their participation in education. For example, Nimrod and Adoni (2006) found in an Israeli national survey of a sample of retired people aged 50–85, that many older people were ill equipped to become actively involved in 'leisure' activities that included attending lectures and classes. Accordingly, these authors stressed the need for more guidance and support, as did Ford (2005). Powell Lawton (1993), drawing on a range of approaches, shows that older people continue to be complex in their orientations and relationships so that their activities also tend to be multidimensional. In addition, later life may bring transitions that impact on relationships, expectations, opportunities and abilities. For example, reduced income, relocation, widowhood, the gradual deterioration of some physical functions or encroaching cognitive impairment may affect willingness and capacity to participate in different types of activities at different times. Szinovacz (1992) found it necessary to combine insights from activity theory with other theoretical perspectives in order to investigate how gender, marital status and household composition relate to social activity patterns after retirement. Finally, activity theory implicitly castigates older people who do not wish to embrace the 'busy' ethic as in some way withdrawn or deviant even though some may quite legitimately prefer more passive pursuits. In general, research on later life has moved on and, as Katz (1996) has shown, has embraced more reliable theories and frameworks within which to examine the lived experiences of older people in their everyday environments.

The moral dimension

Apart from supposed benefits for health and well-being, another approach that can be discerned in many of the writings of educational gerontologists is an emphasis on older people's rights to have access to educational opportunities. This derives mainly from the political economy model of ageing and, in particular, from notions of the relative deprivation of older people in retirement. Although this model may require some modification in view of changing understandings of retirement, it raises important questions about what older people are entitled to expect in their post-work lives (Withnall 2002). Certainly, this approach formed the basis of the 'educational charter for the elderly' published by Laslett (1984), who was closely involved in the genesis of the Forum on the Rights of Elderly People to Education (FREE), a group of enthusiasts in the UK who met during the 1980s to try to raise awareness and interest in the issue and to share information about activities and opportunities (Glendenning 1985). Unfortunately, the Manifesto enshrining these rights published by FREE did not have the long-lasting impact intended at the time and FREE was eventually disbanded. However, Findsen (2005) has observed that the substantial work undertaken by the NIACE *Older and Bolder* programme, discussed earlier, has been largely underpinned by the belief that older people should have a right to educational opportunities in later life.

The moral dimension has also informed other arguments, notably those developed by Schuller and Bostyn (1992) and Carlton and Soulsby (1999). Indeed, Schuller and Bostyn contended that older people should be entitled to educational opportunities as compensation for lack of these earlier in their lives, especially since the divides of gender and class have had such a major impact on the division of educational opportunities for people now in later life.

Reviewing these kinds of approaches, Withnall and Percy (1994) called for something more than just the recognition of educational rights advocated from a quasi-political stance where reasoning is grounded in concepts of equality and justice. They suggested that notions of equal opportunities in the commonly understood sense of the same opportunities for all be abandoned in favour of a focus on the importance of human dignity, on the fulfilment of human potential and the promotion of fair treatment for everyone. However, attempts to ascribe meaning to notions of human dignity and human potential are notoriously difficult. Later, however, Elmore (1999) examined this moral dimension further through a carefully reasoned advocacy of older people's access to both instrumental and expressive education on the basis of social justice but using notions of fair equality of opportunity, access to democratic participation and the status of equal citizenship at a time when many societies are undergoing fundamental change in their social and economic structure. In this way, older people's access to education becomes a tool towards the achievement of a liberal democracy. However, it can be argued that these kinds of discussions have been conducted without reference to the wider debates about ethics and intergenerational equity which have challenged demographers and gerontologists in recent years and forced them to reconsider some long-held assumptions about the sites and boundaries of their disciplinary fields.

Generativity

The theme of intergenerational recognition and reciprocity found expression in both the 1993 European Year of Older People and Solidarity Between Generations and in the 1999 United Nations Year of Older People which took 'towards a society for all ages' as its main slogan. Such an approach derives largely from the work of developmental psychologists such as Erikson (1963), who theorized that human development occurs through a sequence of eight psychosocial stages involving crisis or conflict at each stage. A major developmental crisis is said to occur in early and middle adulthood and to involve the attainment of generativity. This is defined as a concern with others beyond the immediate family, with future generations and the nature of the world in which these descendants will live. People who are successful in resolving this crisis are said to be able to establish clear guidelines for their lives and generally to age in a happy and productive way. Failure to achieve generativity results in stagnation in which people become preoccupied with personal needs, comforts and concerns.

The theme of generativity underpins the work of Laslett (1989), who argued persuasively that self-fulfilment in later life entails those in the so-called Third Age taking responsibility for themselves and their learning and also recognizing the obligation to create an interchange with younger members of society so that an equitable relationship with the future can be secured for the whole of society. Similarly, notions of generativity informed the exploratory work of the American feminist Friedan (1993) in her personal quest to give meaning to the ageing process. It can also be discerned in the vision of 'spiritual eldering' as a creative way of combating the more negative aspects of ageing advocated in the USA by Schachter-Shalomi and Miller (1997). Much of the practical and highly successful intergenerational educational work now taking place in different countries and within some programmes funded by the European Commission bases its *raison d'être* on concepts of generativity (for example, the work discussed by Newman and Hatton-Yeo 2008). We return later to a discussion of intergenerational work.

The 'stages' approach can nevertheless be criticized in that theories of adult development and the personality changes taking place in adulthood that see progression in stages, although influential, have now been largely discredited in that they take insufficient cognizance of class and gender issues and of the changing socio-economic context in which people grow older. Indeed, the sheer diversity of experience in adult life makes it impossible to predict major stages. Crises may occur at any age and may be satisfactorily resolved at individual level with no major effects. Stage theories also imply a discontinuity of development whilst other psychological theories stress the continuity of personality during adulthood. It may well be then, that, whilst participation in educational intergenerational activity might be relevant and rewarding for many older people, these perspectives derived from developmental psychology are inadequate in offering a useful theory that might be translated into practice. Findsen (2005) appears to endorse this conclusion.

A much more promising approach is that of Cohen (2005), who rejected any idea of crisis resolution and preferred to paint a more complex picture of adult development, stressing the enormous creative possibilities of the ageing brain. From his own research, he argued that there are four human potential phases of later life, all of which offer the possibility of growth driven by what he calls 'the Inner Push'. The phases are not necessarily linear but can co-exist and interact. Cohen was able to translate his findings into a list of research-based suggestions for remaining mentally and physically active in later life including participation in lifelong learning.

Critical educational gerontology

The advocacy and development of critical educational gerontology are generally acknowledged to have marked a turning point in thinking about educational opportunities for older people. Formosa has described it as

> [having] emerged from the radical concern to overcome the oppressions which locked older adults into ignorance, poverty and powerlessness, and secondly, as a reaction to the uncritical acceptance of language and the underlying ideological approach employed in older adult education.
>
> (Formosa 2007: 3)

Its appearance as a new theoretical perspective in relation to older adults and their education might originally be ascribed to Phillipson (1983), who had argued that the aim of education in later life should be to illuminate the social and political rights of old age. Allman (1984) was also influential through her claim that the role of education must be to enable learners to be in control of their thinking. The debate was advanced by Battersby (1986), who was commenting somewhat sceptically on the beginnings of the U3A movement in Australia, the introduction of tuition waiver schemes for older people in colleges and universities throughout the United States, the rise of Elderhostel in North America and a network of Colleges for Seniors in Australia and New Zealand, formed with the aim of attracting senior learners from North America to summer schools on the campuses of Australasian universities. The fact that these kinds of initiatives tended to attract older people who had already benefited from the education system led Battersby to question why educators should involve themselves in older adults' continuing education. Like Glendenning, he also wondered whether it is essentially similar to adult education and whether it should be legitimately located within 'lifelong education', which he saw as basically little more than a marketing slogan. He also later asked some pertinent questions about the processes of teaching and learning for older adults, proposing the concept of 'geragogy' as central to understanding 'teaching and learning as a collective and negotiated enterprise amongst older adults' (Battersby 1987: 8–9).

Drawing on the sociological traditions of the Frankfurt school to apply critical theory to educational gerontology, Glendenning and Battersby (1990) began working together to expand these ideas. Their starting point was to challenge what they saw as conventional wisdom in six areas of educational gerontology, i.e. (1) the tendency to regard older people as a relatively homogenous group; (2) the tendency to base programmes for older people on the concept of need, thereby legitimizing the psychological deficit model of older adults' learning abilities; (3) the assumption that education can be an effective intervention strategy for ensuring older people's well-being; (4) the lack of philosophical debate as to why older people should be educated; (5) the belief that education, in whatever mode, is a neutral enterprise and is inherently good for older people; and (6), in view of the marginalization of older people in society, whether the amount of effort spent lobbying for greater access to resources could be justified given the fact that later life education was not on the political agenda. Finally, they referred back to Battersby's original concerns to question whose interests were really being served in promoting and marketing educational programmes for older adults.

They went on to suggest a set of principles that they believed would enable educational gerontologists to think about the future and to consider what should be the aims, objectives and philosophy of educational gerontology. These are summarized in Box 2.1. Later, Battersby (1993) elaborated further on the practical implications of geragogy based on ideas of reflective practice that he believed would enable the voices of educators working with older adults to be heard. Meanwhile, Glendenning continued to raise these issues in subsequent publications (Glendenning 1991, 1997, 2000a). His arguments paralleled and drew on the debates taking place within social gerontology which had also witnessed the gradual emergence of critical perspectives that emphasized the socially constructed nature of ageing and could doubtless be seen partly as a response to the shortcomings of traditional theorizing in the study of later life. It is noticeable that it was also at this point that Glendenning stated that he did not feel it was possible to be an educational gerontologist without also being a social gerontologist (Glendenning 1991).

That his ideas and those of Battersby have resonated with some educators of adults can be seen in various descriptive and analytical accounts of how the possibilities of critical educational gerontology might be explored in practice (e.g. Cusack 1999). Indeed, Formosa (2002) has proposed a set of principles for the practice of critical geragogy largely based on the ideas put forward earlier by Battersby in his radical formulation of older adult teaching and learning as a collective and negotiated enterprise that would

---

Box 2.1   Principles of critical educational gerontology

- A paradigm shift away from functionalism towards a new socio-political framework within which to raise older people's consciousness concerning their right and role within society and to open up a debate between them and the rest of society.
- A move from educational gerontology towards a critical educational gerontology that has its roots in critical social theory and that would address the domestication of older people through an examination of the conventional paradigms concerning theory and practice in later life education.
- The development of a new discourse that would embrace such terms as emancipation, empowerment, transformation, social and hegemonic control and Freire's notion of 'conscientization' usually interpreted as 'consciousness raising'.
- The development of 'praxis', the 'practical articulation' of critical geragogy that would assert that education is not a neutral enterprise and would encourage both older people and educators to question their roles.

(Glendenning and Battersby 1990)

---

articulate the principles of critical educational gerontology. He is nevertheless careful to point out that:

> critical geragogy is neither a system nor is it reducible to any fixed set of proscriptive models. CEG [critical educational gerontology] can only open a frontier of liberating education, which then has to be re-invented and moulded in a sensitive manner in our actual situations, on our own terms and in our own discourses.
>
> (Formosa 2002: 83)

Other critical approaches can be identified within the emerging literature. For example, Findsen, writing as a New Zealander with extensive experience of adult education in both the USA and the UK, discusses the education of older adults drawing on the perspective of political economy to consider aspects of the social and material conditions of older adults' lives and the implications for educational gerontology. His main argument is that, by addressing the social context of older people's lives, educators and other practitioners will gain a better understanding of how those lives can be constrained by social and economic policies and issues of class, gender and ethnicity, issues we have already raised. To this might be added the need to understand the cultural values that influence both the experience of growing older and the nature of learning in later life in different regions (Merriam and Mohamad 2000). Yet, in spite of Findsen's illuminative commentary on the marginalization experienced by older Maori and Pacific people in New Zealand, issues concerning ethnicity and culture in relation to later life educational issues still wait to be critiqued in any depth by researchers, at least in the UK. Findsen goes on to suggest some ways in which educators can begin the process of critical questioning in order to test out their own assumptions and prejudices although his approach is more tentative and not as detailed as that of Formosa discussed above. However, he rightly feels it fair to observe that 'the application of critical theory to this field is in its infancy' (2005: 134) and he succeeds in providing a useful point of departure for continuing debate.

Since then, Formosa has taken the opportunity to develop his own critical perspective on later life education through his work with the University of the Third Age in Valletta, Malta, where it is known as U3E. Here he gives further consideration to issues relating to what he calls 'the intimate connections between older adult education on the one hand and class, culture, and power on the other' (2007: 5). In an interesting adjunct to previous work in critical educational gerontology, he draws on the work of the French sociologist Bourdieu and his concepts of habitus, field and capital to capture and to analyse the motivational aspects of Maltese U3E members' participation in education. From his fieldwork, he concludes firstly, that later life is not devoid of class distinctions and that 'older people are located in structural and subjective class locations which condition them to struggle constantly for improved positions'. Secondly, following Bourdieu, the formation of class and action is characterized by what he calls social investments in and displays of symbolic distinctions. Thirdly, he sees later life education as 'essentially a political activity' and suggests that if associated with a dominant class faction '[it] will form part of a large macrocosm of symbolic institutions that reproduce subtly existing power relations' (2007: 3).

It has to be acknowledged that Formosa bases his conclusions on findings from fieldwork in a particular institution in one unique country. As he explains, there is considerable formal academic control of the U3E in Malta; it is not a self-help organization as in the British U3A model. It may also be the case that he has placed too much emphasis on class to the exclusion of other sources of inequality, a criticism that can be launched at Bourdieu himself. However, Jackson (2006) has also embraced some of the ideas of Bourdieu, arguing from her study of older women learners in a residential college belonging to the National Federation of Women's Institutes (NFWI) in the UK, that analyses of social class should include 'a consideration of the way class identities (including middle-class identities) are (re-) created and perpetuated in different contexts, including through non-formal and informal learning' (Jackson 2006: 85). She notes that the kind of courses on offer at this college served to anchor students in choices that were located in both social class and gender expectations about women's traditional roles. Whilst they offered women the advantages of a women-only learning space, she argues that learning can also be a mechanism for exclusion. The issues she raises are certainly worthy of further consideration especially in relation to learning that takes place outside a formal context; this is not addressed in Formosa's analysis.

Gender issues in later life education

Jackson's work is very useful in that it begins to locate debate within a different framework. However, a number of other commentators have also adopted a critical perspective by turning their attention to gender issues in later life education and learning, although much of the current debate relates specifically to older women. Of course, women are more numerous in the senior population owing to their comparative longevity and, since they tend to form the majority in formally organized courses and classes, they may be easier to locate for research purposes. Yet it has been found that they somehow tend to be less visible within a mixed classroom where male learners are more likely to dominate any discussion even when in the minority (Bunyan and Jordan 2005; de Medeiros *et al.* 2007), a finding that would also merit further empirical exploration.

It is interesting to note that Formosa (2005), who identifies himself as a white male but as a feminist, has also begun to consider this approach. Apart from his formulation of the principles of critical geragogy and his later interest in class issues, he has previously discussed the ways in which critical educational gerontology can be embedded within a feminist perspective. His starting point was that critical educational gerontology, as it has been developed, represents yet another patriarchal discourse where women are silenced or made passive. Again arising from his fieldwork with the University of the Third Age in Malta, he proposed five principles to assist later life education to become a means of transformative education for older women. These are shown in Box 2.2.

Box 2.2   Principles of transformative education for older women

- Acknowledge them as an oppressed population as a result of the double standard of ageing.
- Focus on women's cumulative lifelong disadvantages.
- Reject any idea of a single female identity and embrace a 'politics of difference'.
- Focus on a feminist praxis in both older people's education and in related research.
- Drive towards the empowerment of women as a distinct but collective effort.

To some extent, his views echo the earlier ideas of Hiemstra, an American male academic who also considered himself 'a feminist and an enthusiastic supporter of feminist values, causes and initiatives' (1993: 3). Hiemstra argued, mainly from his own extensive experience, that whilst older women differ from older men as learners they also differ from younger women in a number of ways. He suggested a series of policies for educationalists to adopt in respect of older women learners and devised various implementation strategies based on findings about images of them although these were largely gleaned from selected American research studies on adult learners from the 1980s.

To a degree, this emphasis on older women as learners is to be welcomed. However, it can be argued that it runs the risk not just of seeing all older women as similarly oppressed but also of categorizing older men as a homogeneous group of confident individuals already well served by educational provision and thereby obscuring complex issues of male diversity, beliefs and motivation. Together with Jackson's findings (2006) previously discussed, an Australian study by Golding *et al.* (2007) of an attempt to cater for hard-to-reach and isolated men, many of whom were over 65, through the informal and practical approaches of 'men's sheds' raises some questions about the role of separate educational provision for older men and women. For example, does such provision help to challenge possible stereotypical beliefs of both practitioners and older learners themselves concerning gender roles and appropriate modes of behaviour in an educational setting or does it merely endorse existing prejudices? How does it impact on teaching and learning processes? To what extent do the findings of Golding and his colleagues also have implications for feminist theory and for critical approaches? As yet, there are no easy answers.

Although undertaken in a different Australian context, Williamson's (2000) work on gender issues also arises from concerns about the comparative absence of men from later life learning opportunities. On the basis of his in-depth study of one U3A campus in a suburb of Sydney, he argues that the imbalance of men and women at least in this U3A reflects a range of issues including gender role socialization, resulting in differing perceptions of retirement and different kinds of interests, marital status, health and social group membership as well as associated practical barriers such as lack of transport. He also suggests that some older men do not wish to be involved with organizations that they perceive to be dominated by women, an issue on which Golding *et al.* (2007) also comment in relation to men's perceived need for a space not primarily designed for and by women. However, Williamson is careful to emphasize, firstly, that not enough is really understood about the highly individual paths that men and women follow in retirement. Secondly, the differing experiences and expectations of subsequent cohorts may result in substantial changes to the scenario he has described (Williamson 2000).

Moving on: hearing the voices of older learners

Critical approaches to post-work education have drawn attention to the ways in which later life is increasingly characterized by widening inequalities largely determined by the socio-economic structure and implicated with issues of class, gender, ethnicity, culture and, indeed, age itself although only class and gender have so far been explored in any depth. We would also argue for the need to take more account of psychological evidence concerning the impact of ageing on health status and lifestyles and on any observable differences between the comparatively fit and active majority of older people and the minority suffering acute or chronic illness or experiencing cognitive impairment. However, critical approaches have themselves been critiqued. Early in the debate, Percy (1990) argued forcibly for the continuation of a humanistic perspective on later life education in which all individuals, their perspectives, experience and potential as an educational resource for their peers and other generations should be valued in the interests of all. Yet Withnall has previously commented, following Usher *et al.* (1997), that both the humanistic and the critical approaches fall into the trap of regarding older people as a homogeneous group and risk imposing a new kind of ideological constraint (Withnall 2000). Findsen (2005) asks for a closer examination of how theory and practice in critical educational gerontology might be better integrated and also raises questions as to how it connects with the concept of lifelong learning. Formosa reports his own doubts about the critical approach that he sees as allied to a traditional view of social power and with a tendency to 'link the notion of domination with the materiality of economic forces' (2007: 5).

Formosa has succeeded in extending the debate through his espousal of a Bourdieusian approach but we would argue that educational gerontology is still grappling to some extent with notions of power, empowerment and disempowerment, an issue that Findsen (2005) also addresses. There is sometimes still a tacit assumption that education will automatically 'empower' older people and reduce their perceived social exclusion, a position adopted by Kump and Krašovec (2007) in their work with older people in Slovenia. Yet, almost two decades ago, community educators were already struggling to clarify what they meant by 'power' within education, arguing that it is not a tangible entity to be given or received. It can exist only within a relationship that may be relatively simple or, conversely, highly complex. In addition, individuals within groups often seen by educators as powerless may in fact possess considerable power within other networks in which they operate so it is probably too much of a generalization to talk of people as completely 'powerless' or as having been 'disempowered'. What is important is the balance of power within each relationship, and this depends largely on the resources available within that relationship. Such resources may be physical but may also consist of experience, knowledge, skills, self-confidence and a sense of solidarity. Accordingly, although educators are unlikely to be able to challenge institutional power or even redistribute power on their own, they can try to increase the resources available to those who appear to be lacking power in a particular relationship through the processes of educational engagement (O'Hagan 1991), a position at which Findsen (2005) also appears to have arrived. As he points out, this approach is necessary for the achievement of more equitable power relations; it may be a more appropriate long-term goal for educators rather than a narrower focus on issues of 'power with' or 'power to' as proposed by Cusack (1999).

In the previous chapter, it was suggested that what is needed is to relocate the debate from *education* and the concerns of the provider and practitioner to *learning* and to focus on older people themselves, whether they currently identify themselves as learners or not. To date, research that has incorporated the voices of older people themselves has been partial and fragmented with the result that we have a relatively poor understanding of what learning means to older people and the role it plays in their lives, issues that our study was designed to address. In the next chapter, we turn to description and analysis of the first stage of our study, a series of ten focus group discussions held with older learners in very different formal educational settings in different parts of the UK.

Conclusion

Over the last three decades or so, there has been considerable debate concerning education and older people originating in the USA where awareness of the ageing population and the implications for providers of learning opportunities was apparent in the early 1970s. The emergence of educational gerontology and attempts to give it meaning and definition were initially of interest; recent years have seen the influence of a critical gerontology and the growing influence of postmodern and feminist approaches. Here we have advocated a move from previous emphases on education to an exploration of what learning itself means in the lives of older learners and the role it plays for them post-work as a preliminary to discussing our study in more detail.

Part II

What does the research tell us?

Chapter 3

What has influenced later life learners?

Introduction

Here we will discuss the processes and findings of the first stage of our research, which consisted of focus group interviews. These were carried out with ten groups of older people currently involved in different formally organized learning programmes. The aim in this initial stage was, firstly, to identify any shared perceptions of the historical and social contexts of their lives and the characteristics of participants' involvement with education and with learning activities during their lives together with current forms of engagement with learning. Secondly, it was planned to use the findings to formulate a conceptual model of the various influences on learning that could then be tested with both current learners and non-learners in the second stage of the research. We will also reflect on the issues that arose in the course of completing this initial stage and discuss the implications for the next and subsequent stages.

The decision to use focus group interviews in this first stage of the research requires some comment. Kitzinger and Barbour (1999) claim that focus groups can be distinguished from the broader category of group interviews by the explicit use of group interaction to generate data. Indeed, focus groups have increased in popularity as an additional tool for qualitative researchers in recent years across a range of professional enquiries, especially in health and nursing research (McLafferty 2004). There is also evidence of their use in educational research (e.g. Wilson 1997) and, in particular, in researching lifelong learning issues, as Field (2000) has shown. His own experience of conducting focus groups for this purpose suggests that they can be a useful way of involving end-users in research, an overall aim in this particular work with older learners. Although he does not claim that focus groups represent any serious challenge to what he calls 'methodological individualism' in lifelong learning, he also believes that they offer 'a useful way of actively involving and engaging with the agendas of those who are being researched; of exploring their shared everyday experiences, values and orientations; and witnessing the nature of relationships between individuals' (Field 2000: 334).

Although it was also planned here to use focus groups to explore a facet of lifelong learning, an additional concern for the research was that participants would be asked to recall and reflect upon their experiences of learning across the life course as well as discussing aspects of their current involvement. Wallace (1994) discusses in detail some of the issues that scholars have raised in relation to using such an approach. For example, he argues that life stories are necessarily subjective interpretations and evaluations that may be subject to reinterpretation over time and in different contexts. Alternatively, they may be seen as social constructions that are created and sustained by social interaction and that are made real only through telling and presentation. In a situation where participants would be recalling specific aspects of their lives, it would be important to be aware of issues of validity and reliability in the accounts they offered as well as being open to what Chioncel *et al.* have termed a tendency towards 'groupthink' in focus group discussions (2003: 496). Indeed, members of the research team were aware of the dangers of forcing focus group members to reach a consensus on any particular issues and, from the outset, intended to be open and alert to different perspectives and the ways in which they were expressed.

Bearing in mind the above issues, the research team sought to carry out discussions with groups of older people who were currently involved with some kind of learning activity formally organized by an external body. Activities organized by older people themselves under the auspices of, for example, the University of the Third Age were also eligible for inclusion. This did not preclude the fact that some of the potential focus group participants may have also been learning in more than one formal setting or, indeed, pursuing an individual learning interest alone or informally with friends or relatives. How groups were located and contacted and the issues involved are described in the Appendix. A typology is presented in Box 3.1.

Box 3.1   Focus groups: type and location

Further Education College based	North Midlands
University based	Scotland
Senior Forum (voluntary)	South East
Retired people's group (voluntary)	East Midlands
Charitable association	North Midlands
University of the Third Age group	Wales
Community group	London
Ethnic minority community association	West Midlands
Residential home based	North West
Voluntary group organized by national charity	Eastern England

Data collection and analysis

In total, 98 older people were present for the ten focus group discussions. It is apparent that group size may have an impact on how discussion unfolds and it was also noted that focus group size as reported in the literature tends to range from around six to ten participants with smaller numbers recommended for older people (Quine 1998). Group size here ranged from five to twenty-two participants with a mean of nine. In the very large group, every older person attending activities in the building on the day wanted to be present, and the size meant that it was not a focus group in the accepted sense. However, no more than ten people actually participated in the discussion whilst the others indicated that they were there to observe and listen. Gender ratios were not recorded for this larger group but within the remaining groups 70 per cent of members were female. Each discussion lasted for an average of two hours, considerably longer than expected. In some cases, participants were keen to continue beyond this, but others were anxious to get home or to keep other appointments so that discussions were generally brought to a close after this time.

Although ethical issues had been covered in the original material supplied to the organizations, all participants were asked to read and sign a statement to the effect that they understood the purposes of the research and the use to which the data collected would be put as well as assuring them of confidentiality and anonymity at all times They were also asked to spend some minutes prior to the main discussion considering and agreeing a set of written ground rules that included the need to confine debate to the immediate context and to respect other participants' rights to be heard and their points of view together with the right to withdraw from the group at any stage. Attention was also paid to preferred forms of address (Quine 1998), although in all cases participants were happy with informal use of given names.

In recording the focus groups' deliberations, it was decided not to rely only on taped versions of the discussions since tapes cannot adequately pick up all verbal behaviour in a large room or record body language. Some participants also made it clear that they would feel inhibited by the knowledge that their comments were being recorded (although two groups did happily consent). Instead, the moderator made detailed notes throughout and briefly fed back the main points made prior to moving to a new question, also seeking participants' assent that this summary reflected accurately the issues that had been discussed. Where they were available, flip charts were used to record important points and as an aide-memoire. On the basis of the notes made in the reporting forms, individual focus group summary reports were then produced and sent to all participants as soon as possible after the focus group had taken place. They were asked to read these carefully and to validate that the main issues that arose in their focus group discussions had been accurately identified and fairly reported prior to more detailed analysis. Comments received were incorporated into new versions of the summaries in two cases.

Because of the complexities of analysing focus group data, a systematic approach to uncovering themes from the discussion was used (Frankland and Bloor 1999), taking into account the context in which each group discussion took place and the composition of the group. The summaries were analysed manually, as it was considered that software packages would be inappropriate, particularly as in interpreting the data constant reference was made to the team's observational field notes relating to any sensitive topics raised, how these were addressed and the language used by participants.

Findings

Guided by the interview questions, the ten focus groups discussed the historical, social and cultural contexts of their lives together with their experiences of learning during childhood, in early adulthood and mid-life as well as during the post-work period. Although all the groups acknowledged that historical events and social changes would have been experienced differently especially in view of group members' different ages, each group collectively identified a range of what they saw as important influences. Here we will comment briefly on the main themes that emerged and that were used to build a conceptual model and to inform the next stages of the research.

The context: experiencing disruption and change

The groups began their discussions by identifying and discussing the various changes they perceived to have taken place during their lives. Although it appeared that there was considerable variation in ages within each group, the Second World War and its aftermath were seen by all groups both as the most important event they had experienced and/or as the catalyst that had set other changes in motion. However, most focus group participants had been children or teenagers at the time and recalled the war mainly in terms of the messages they had received from parents to the effect that 'things had been different' in the recent past. Others, who had experienced the war years as adults, chose to discuss it in a broader historical context, pointing out that, in some areas, there had actually been many years of hardship prior to the war with very little work available. However, all the groups recalled the sense of disruption to their lives, whether they had been children who experienced evacuation or adults whose war service interfered with family, jobs and education. A few participants had suffered loss and bereavement. Overall, there was considerable emphasis on a remembered sense of impermanence in society at this time and a corresponding feeling of immediacy in life generally.

In spite of this, some groups moved on to consider more positive aspects of the war and its aftermath. National Service, although also seen as a major cause of disruption of family life, was considered by some older male group participants to have given people the opportunity to break away from traditional social expectations. This was achieved largely through the chance to learn new skills or attend training courses that eventually took them in a different direction. The chance to meet people from all over the country when they were based away from home and becoming aware that the better educated 'lived on a different planet' were seen as motivational factors for some participants. Both male and female participants in one group observed that, in spite of some immediate postwar difficulties caused mainly by rationing, their generation had 'had things a lot better than our parents'.

These discussions led the groups on to consider more broadly the structural changes in society that they perceived the war to have initially set in motion. The family, and in particular the economic position of women together with changing concepts of childhood, were considered at length by all groups, together with observations about expectations of, and changes in, the workplace and what was seen as the current lack of security in employment. However, there was general agreement that it was during the 1960s that, as one female participant commented 'society became dark, demanding and uncaring'. This period was seen as a time when the media became powerful and people had access to unprecedented amounts of information, resulting, it was felt, in social comparison and a growth in materialism. Participants also observed that it was also a time when people began to travel abroad more for holidays so that their cultural horizons were broadened considerably during this decade.

All the groups were especially concerned about reasons for observed changes in family structures and these were analysed in some depth, with several members of one group choosing to share personal stories of the break-up of their own, their children's or other relatives' marriages. There was less agreement among the groups regarding the changing position of women, and debate in some groups became very forceful. Some people thought that, even though women had worked during the war, there had still been constraints on their career prospects and professional advancement; now they had been enabled to fulfil their potential and to demonstrate their strengths. Others, including some female participants themselves, disagreed and were concerned that women 'had become more like men' with changes in dress codes, traditional gender roles and behaviour and what was seen as a consequent loss of femininity.

All the groups were anxious to comment on the growth of technology and the increase in the amount and nature of information available as well as observing that life today has become even more materialistic with the pressures of consumerism that they saw as largely fuelled by television. A common example was the pressure children were felt to place on parents to purchase desirable but expensive items. This led on to lengthy discussions about changes in child rearing practices and the perceived lack of discipline and respect apparent in children's behaviour today even though children were largely seen as being 'over-protected'. Here some group members again shared experiences from their own families. Although not everyone in each group was always in agreement with the majority views, what emerged from these initial discussions was a perceived sense of continuing structural and operational change and discontinuity in society and, consequently, in people's lives. However, participants generally expressed agreement that the onus was on them to find ways of maintaining a sense of personal continuity and to cope by keeping abreast of changes whether these were in society at large or impinged at a personal level. It was felt particularly important to accept that nowadays 'young people do things differently' especially with regard to shifting family structures and child rearing practices. There was little sense of any ability to resist or to challenge change.

Situational influences on access to education and learning

A second theme that emerged related to situational factors both collective and individual that impacted on group members' access to education and opportunities to learn at all stages of their lives. It has already been seen that the Second World War was viewed both negatively as having disrupted some people's education and positively in the sense of having opened up a range of new opportunities for others. However, all the groups traced an intangible sense of growing uncertainty and an inability to control the major events that have come to affect people's lives on a daily basis so that situational influences were seen as operating within the broader context of both historical events and continuing unpredictable social and cultural change.

Acknowledging this point, members of all the groups put considerable emphasis on the situational influence of family expectations and individual life events on their education and access to learning opportunities, both those formally organized and those undertaken on an informal basis. These were seen as intertwined particularly with issues of gender and perceived class. For example, many of the women participants had been unable to continue their initial education past the age of 14, with one woman explaining that it was a case of 'boys – to be educated; girls – marriage or work'. Even in relation to the adult world of work, there was general agreement that 'women were held back' and that there was 'no expectation for women to take anything other than mundane jobs'. The impact of these expectations was a major issue for those women who described their origins as working-class and whose fathers, in particular, had assumed that 'education was a waste of time for girls'.

In adult life, memories of parental expectations combined with changing socio-economic influences and personal circumstances tended to influence working lives and the kinds of opportunities available for learning that were often work-related. At this point, several more members of the groups chose to illustrate the issues with some quite personal experiences of divorce or early widowhood. Ironically, adverse personal circumstances, especially for women, had sometimes resulted in a few individuals in the groups going on to carve out professional careers as teachers or nurses out of sheer financial necessity in spite of early negative parental expectations. Most of the other women had not worked since starting a family or had stayed in the same local industry for years so that 'learning on the job' was the main way in which they had accessed learning, if at all. Many of the men had also remained with the same company or organization during their working lives although they were more likely to have had formal opportunities for work-based learning of different kinds and for continuing professional development, especially the few who had entered higher education and then followed professional careers. However, it was also stressed by one man that 'work came first' and there would have been very little time to pursue any individual learning interests, a view strongly confirmed in other groups.

The ethnic minority focus group members, most of whom had been born outside the UK, had very little to say about situational influences on their earlier lives. It was not clear whether they had simply forgotten their early experiences or felt that their memories had no relevance to the discussion. It may have been that they simply did not feel comfortable at being asked to contribute to a discussion involving personal histories or lacked confidence in their oral skills to the extent that they were unable to express their views within a group. However, in common with some members of other groups, they were more forthcoming when discussing the range of activities they were involved in post-work even though they did not necessarily identify this as 'learning'.

Indeed, at this point in the discussions, all the groups began to question and reconsider their unspoken assumptions about the meanings that can be ascribed to learning. What emerged was a general agreement that learning is actually something more than what had been experienced through formal education earlier in life and includes being able to update existing skills or to develop new ones or to take part in 'leisure learning' including sports and exercise, and to pursue individual interests whether these are intellectual or creative or both. At this point some members of the groups that were based in towns or cities revealed that they actually took part in a varied range of activities, often attending different types of institution on different days of the week. Those able to afford it also talked enthusiastically of informal learning through travel undertaken during retirement, since long-haul flights were now cheaper and distant countries more accessible. Other group members mentioned independent learning projects on which they had embarked or various forms of charity or volunteer work that also involved incidental learning. Indeed, a group taking part in self-help co-operative learning moved its discussion on to a broader consideration of how older people could have their substantial contribution to society as learners, volunteers and unpaid carers valued and recognized rather than always 'having things done for us'.

One group agreed on the phrase 'indulgent learning' to illustrate how learning activity in later life, which is usually self-chosen, differs from the 'compulsory learning' undertaken earlier in life, which had frequently been prescribed by others and in which there was little sense of individual choice or control. This change of perceptions of learning and the decision to become involved seems to have been closely connected not only to the realization of having more time available in the post-work phase of life but also to the actual timing of becoming post-work, the reasons for it and subsequent situational circumstances. Time to pursue own interests resulted from having been freed from the substantial demands of earning a living and raising a family and, in a few cases, through release from the responsibility of caring for a relative who had now died. These kinds of changes occurred at different ages for different participants and were often preceded by a complex chain of events that had left little time for forward planning. Even those who had made definitive plans for the post-work period of their lives reported that these had not always worked out but that other unexpected opportunities had sometimes materialized.

Practical challenges such as needing to cope with various life changes or to rebuild a life were thus cited as examples of some of the situational factors that had encouraged later life learning. However, these needs were frequently underpinned by less tangible desires such as being able to maintain a positive outlook or to find meaning in life. These factors were particularly relevant for the focus group participants living in a residential home. The chance to take part in a learning activity was welcomed in that it also offered a change in environment and an opportunity to interact with other residents, both of which were seen as crucial in staying positive.

Institutional influences on education and learning

The third theme to emerge, which generated some of the most animated discussion, was concerned with the impact on people's experiences of education and learning of the various institutions with which participants had been involved or associated over their lives. It was noticeable that perceptions of learning at primary school were generally very positive. A clear majority in the groups felt they had received 'a good basic education' with excellent teachers, although some participants again referred to disruption caused by evacuation and mixed-age classes where individual needs were not catered for. Most groups agreed that parental and community support for school and respect for teachers as well as a sense of security and a clear structure underpinned by strong discipline were key influences. However, one group discussed this last issue at length, concluding that their childhood experiences of discipline had represented nothing less than adult violence in a form that would certainly not be tolerated today; accordingly, they spent some time debating acceptable limits of discipline.

There was less agreement about teaching methods such as rote learning which, although making it easier for some children to learn, had made it impossible for others. There had also been no recognition of special learning needs caused by such conditions that would now be recognised as, for example, dyslexia, with one man recalling that 'I was called backward, stupid, thick'. Neither were the difficulties encountered in learning to write by those who were left-handed properly addressed. Rather, it was recalled that displaying ambition and pride in achievements were mainly seen as the keys to success. Competitiveness, which participants felt was no longer encouraged in schools today, was also considered to be a motivational factor.

There was generally less enthusiasm for secondary school where, although there were some clear individual memories of particular teachers who loved their subject and had sparked enthusiasm in some participants, poor or bored teachers who were felt to lack interest in helping children to learn had played a part in discouraging interest in learning for many. In discussion, societal restrictions on married women remaining in teaching and the conscription of those who might have trained as teachers during the war were identified by some groups as possible explanations for the presence in some schools of some very poor teachers. The issue of financial problems in staying on at school, coupled with the gender-based expectations of teachers as well as those of parents, also had a negative influence on memories of secondary education, especially for the women participants.

During adulthood, in addition to the opportunities available to those who had undertaken National Service, learning had taken place in a variety of institutions. These had included full-time study at university or teacher training college for a few, but had mainly consisted of day release at technical college under apprenticeship schemes, through night school classes (some men recalled attending two or three evenings a week) or short courses based in the workplace and again mainly attended by the male respondents. Some participants had tried to gain further qualifications or to generally improve themselves through financing their own study at adult education classes. There were commonly held perceptions that educational institutions that offered qualifications had nevertheless demanded a considerable commitment of time and effort from students seeking to obtain them, considered far in excess of what seems to be required today. Some of the women in one group talked about how they had gained qualifications outside educational institutions through non-formal organizations such as the Girl Guides. The local public library as a catalyst for informal learning was important to those who had lived in urban areas and was considered by one enthusiastic user as 'one of the best things in this country – its lifeblood'. These views triggered a range of other memories of ways of learning informally, and most of the participants were able to supply other examples.

In discussing the impact of institutions and organizations on the learning in which they were currently engaged, the groups mainly returned to consideration of issues of location and accessibility leading to a broader discussion of the various practical barriers formal educational institutions were seen to put in the way of older learners, often combined with transport difficulties, especially in rural areas. At a practical level, the actual decision to take the important first step was often related to familiar institutional factors such as physical accessibility, low costs and convenient timing of classes or courses so that participants did not have to be out after dark and, more importantly in some cases, face returning to an empty house alone. Many of the ethnic minority group members were both collected and returned home by minibus but 'having someone to go with' when first attending a course or class was an important situational factor, especially for many of the women in other groups. There was appreciation from all the community-based groups that they had been able to find appropriate provision that took account of their varying interests and preferred timing as well as offering ease of location and understanding of the need for costs to be low. Individuals in nine of the ten groups cited the choice of activities, flexibility in teaching and learning methods, the absence of exams plus the time and opportunity to maintain or build a social network that contrasted strongly with their experiences of institutionally based learning earlier in adulthood.

There was keen awareness that these opportunities were not always available in many other areas of the UK. In fact, two groups emphasized the vision and untiring efforts of named educational professionals in fighting for, and helping to set up, specific provision for older people under the auspices of their various employer institutions. This was seen as particularly important in areas where there were few other appropriate facilities for older people in that they were also offered the chance to socialize and make new friends. At this point, participants in the tenth group began to discuss the extent to which their mostly creative and practical interests that tended to be pursued on an individual basis could be considered as learning at all. For them, the social benefits of attendance appeared to have assumed more importance. However, three groups stressed that learning was definitely the main objective of their attendance, and their members felt that the social benefits were a welcome additional bonus.

For the group living in a residential care home, there was a sense in which this institution appeared to restrict their learning activities. Although the home enjoyed the comparative luxury of a full-time activities organizer, it was not clear to what extent she received adequate funding or tutor support to be able to offer the range of activities that some of the residents would have liked. However, they did not comment directly on this and were appreciative of the facilities available.

In these very lengthy and sometimes heated discussions, there was a strong acknowledgement that the schools and other types of institutions and organizations that provided educational opportunities for group participants at different points in their lives were themselves products of a changing historical, socio-economic and cultural context, and both the type and nature of provision available at any given time and their experiences as learners reflected their own and wider societal values. With the more recent acknowledgement of the importance of lifelong learning in educational policy circles, some group participants were optimistic that, in future, there would be wider recognition of the importance of offering better educational opportunities to older people. In this way, the sense of continuing external change and its effects again came to dominate some of the discussions.

Individual Influences

The fourth theme to emerge related specifically to individual influences on, and attitudes to learning, especially the likelihood of individuals incorporating learning activity, broadly defined, into their post-work life. Initially, groups again referred to negative institutional influences that might have impacted on individuals' attitudes to learning and still discourage them from being vitally engaged. The possible effects of other negative factors such as poor health and depression in later life also received some consideration at this point although rather less than might have been expected. However, in two of the larger focus groups, there was very strong agreement that people who engage with any form of learning post-work exhibit certain positive personality traits. These include 'determination', 'guts', 'courage' and they are also likely to possess 'an inquisitive and alert mind' whatever their personal circumstances and the situational, institutional and other barriers that may be put in their way. Some of these group participants claimed to have been aware that they possessed these characteristics at an early age and that their lifelong love of learning had consequently emerged during early childhood. Even less positive learning experiences or the expectations of others at different points in the life course had failed to deflect them. This was particularly the case for the women who had been forced to support themselves financially in adult life although it was not entirely clear how far they might be interpreting an external pressure in terms of their own personality traits. Others reflected that situational factors later in adult life had encouraged them to turn to joining a class or course initially for social or other reasons but that their enjoyment of learning had become paramount and they had come to discover new aspects of their personalities at a later stage. One of these participants also likened learning to 'ripples on a pond'. She suggested that, once an individual makes a decision to learn something, its effects spread out to and permeate all other areas of that person's life.

Two groups were highly critical of other older people they knew who 'moaned about their lives' which appeared to have very little focus but who made no effort to get involved in any activities or to try anything new. There was little acceptance of possible situational or external barriers in these older people's lives and a strongly expressed belief that later life offers considerable opportunities to face new challenges. Although this positive view was by no means universally held among the groups, it did reinforce the notion of taking personal responsibility for coping with change that had emerged earlier on.

Emerging issues

The use of focus groups

The focus group discussions were wide-ranging and occupied a con-siderable amount of time in the early stages of the research. Because of the very different backgrounds, circumstances and experiences of the people who took part, it was not surprising that the discussions did not always proceed in a similar fashion. In some cases, individual participants tried to dominate discussion, expressing views very forcefully. Others were more guarded in what they said, sometimes worrying that they were offering an opinion that they knew was 'probably not politically correct', suggesting an awareness of the changed social environment. In some groups, participants were happy to reveal personal aspects of their lives that were obviously difficult or painful whilst others in the groups were more reticent in what they were willing to discuss.

The role of the moderator both as a facilitator and as part of the audience for the discussion has received considerable attention in the emerging literature on focus groups (Kitzinger and Barbour 1999). In these focus groups, perceptions of age, academic background, dress and manner of speaking meant that members of the research team who were acting as moderators may have been seen as 'outsiders' within the different focus groups. In the ethnic minority group, it was not clear whether the identity of their moderator as a young white female academic had any specific impact on the level of the group's willingness to engage in dialogue both with her and with each other but it may have added to their comparative reticence (Chiu and Knight 1999). Conversely, moderators themselves were occasionally puzzled by discussion of particular past events of which they had little personal knowledge; or they did not fully understand some largely obsolete phrases that were used quite naturally in conversation by some focus group member. These concerns were addressed through regular team debriefings and through theorizing the researcher's role in the overall research process.

Nevertheless, using a life course perspective and encouraging reflection and group discussion enabled a preliminary insight to emerge into some of the main influences on participants' experiences of education and learning within the wider framework of historical events and major societal and cultural changes. Certainly, the sense of disruption and dislocation in society that participants recalled in their early lives appears to have remained with them, but a majority displayed progressive attitudes towards change and emphasized the importance of acceptance and of taking personal responsibility for coping with it. Indeed, a Dutch study has also challenged the commonly held belief that older adults are conservative in their views and shows how major changes in society have affected older people's opinions (Poortman and Van Tilburg 2005).

Identified situational influences included the expectations of parents and family earlier in life combined with individual life events. However, the sense of self-reliance and the emphasis on respect, pride, competitiveness and personal achievement that most of the groups recalled from childhood educational experiences may be key factors in encouraging them to learn in later life even though, for some groups, the social aspect was paramount. Some participants' claims to possess the kind of personality traits that helped them to be committed learners might be questioned in the light of more recent findings that it may well be experiences of learning itself that impact positively on different aspects of psychological and mental health provided that learning provision has matched the interests, strengths and needs of the learner (Hammond 2004). It was apparent that members of those groups who recalled very positive experiences of primary school were also those who claimed to possess the characteristics required of lifelong learners.

Jarvis (1994) has explored the notion that people's biographies are largely moulded through their learning experiences and suggests that the amount of learning to which they expose themselves may well change as they age. His theoretical perspective may account for the difficulties some of the groups encountered in trying to ascribe a meaning to learning in later life. He was able to construct a typology of responses to potential learning experiences based on the relationship between biography and experience. Among the focus group respondents, it was possible to identify a majority of those whom he terms 'sages': these are older people who are aware that there is still much to learn and are eager to continue. A large number of 'doers' who may also be sages but who are additionally engaged in a very wide range of activities including sport and travel also emerged. Those older people who were perceived to be doing nothing by some group members may well be described as 'anomics', those who cannot learn from their experiences because the disjuncture between their biography and their experience is too great. At the same time, we were also aware of a number of 'harmony seekers' within the groups – those who seek to live in accord with their surroundings and to create a secure environment for themselves because they have achieved peace of mind and so may wish to limit their learning. To some extent, this applied to the residential home group members but it is not clear how far this might have been due to force of circumstance and lack of opportunity to expand their learning activities because of other constraints.

A conceptual model

After consideration of the broad themes that emerged, we were able to devise a conceptual model of the life course incorporating the possible influences on these older adults' learning experiences to the point at which they were currently involved in learning (Figure 3.1). The essence of the model is the use of the notion of time to try to construct links between biography and the social structure (Blaikie 1999). It is shown how the multiplicity of influences on the collective and individual life course operate in an interrelated but highly complex manner within a continually changing and evolving social and cultural context; and how the individual is affected by situational, institutional and personal factors to influence the timing and circumstances of becoming post-work and the possibilities of subsequent involvement in learning. Changing and differing notions of what constitutes 'learning' as people grow older also expressed by participants were an important outcome of the discussions and are represented here. The model also had the potential to incorporate findings regarding the perceived outcomes of learning post-work that were to be investigated in more detail at a later stage of the research.

In reflecting on the focus group discussions and in formulating the model, it quickly became apparent that the adoption of a life course approach poses considerable methodological problems. For example, it was almost impossible to unravel completely the very complex interplay of individual characteristics and personality factors and the variety of individual and collective experiences over a lifetime combined with possible genetic and environmental influences on the processes of growing up and growing older (Bergeman 1997) that a holistic life course analysis would properly require. However, the approach enabled a very rich data set to be obtained and provided opportunities for the older learners involved in the focus groups to begin to make their own links between different aspects of their life experiences and the changing social structure over time. From informal comments made to the researchers outside the focus groups, it also became clear that the older people who participated were generally happy to be approached and enjoyed the experience of contributing to a study that addressed issues they saw as relevant to their lives but that had not previously attracted much attention from the research community.

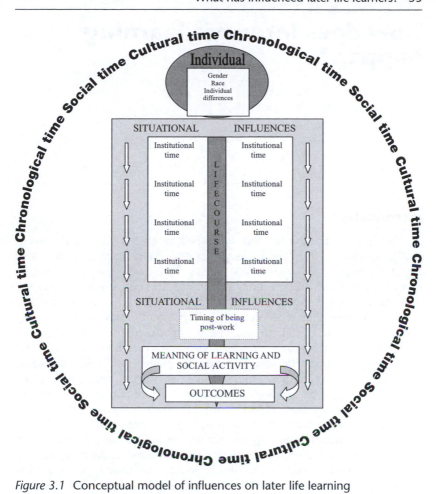

Figure 3.1 Conceptual model of influences on later life learning

Conclusion

Focus groups proved to be a useful interactive tool for introducing our study to groups of older learners and offered them the opportunity to tell us about their lives. The themes that emerged enabled us to construct a model that represented the issues raised during the discussion and that could be used in the next stages of the research. The immediate aim was to test the validity of the conceptual model with different groups of older learners also currently learning in some kind of formal organization together with a number of other older people not so involved. This is discussed in the next chapter.

Chapter 4

How does later life learning happen?

Introduction

In this third stage of the research we aimed, firstly, to examine the issues that had emerged from the focus group discussions in more depth with larger and more diverse groups of older people through a more detailed investigation of their backgrounds and experiences of learning during their lives. Secondly, we now wanted to start moving the focus of the study to the kinds of learning that people undertake in later life and the choices they make about it and to begin to make sense of their experiences of learning. This would enable us to reconsider the model that had emerged from the focus group discussions. Accordingly, we planned to explore the backgrounds of a further sample of older people who were currently taking part in a formally organized educational course or class ('participants') and an additional group not currently so involved ('non-participants') although we acknowledged that members of the latter group might consider themselves to be learning within other types of settings or indeed learning informally in some other way. A mailed questionnaire was chosen as the most suitable instrument for data collection in that it would allow us to access a greater number of older people. Details of the sampling frame, the methods used to locate both 'participants' and 'non-participants' and the procedures adopted in the administration of the questionnaires and analysis of the data obtained are discussed in detail in the Appendix. The questions to be explored arose mainly from the issues raised in the focus groups and were designed to reflect this. It should also be noted that, in the discussion of the findings below, percentages have been rounded and so may not always total 100 per cent.

As previously, we did not define what we meant by 'learning' at the outset although we did explain what we meant by 'formal' and 'informal' aspects. Our hope was that respondents' own definitions would emerge. To facilitate their thinking on this issue, they were also invited to complete a sentence beginning '*Learning is . . .*' and to offer any further comments they wished at the end of the questionnaire about their life course experiences of education and learning. As the questionnaire was quite lengthy and required not only the ability to recall past life events but also considerable thought and reflection, we were surprised by the effort many respondents made to set down their views in detail. We have therefore drawn extensively on this additional qualitative data to further illuminate the quantitative findings.

Findings

Respondents' backgrounds

Of the 100 questionnaires mailed (50 to 'participants' and 50 to 'non-participants'), 77 older people responded (77 per cent). Of those, 38 were involved in some kind of formally organized learning at the time of completion and 39 were not so involved. Respondents' characteristics are shown in Table 4.1.

It is worth noting that, in general, these questionnaire respondents appeared to be rather older than the focus group members although this may be largely coincidental; or it may be indicative of the kinds of organizations from which participant respondents were recruited. If this was the case, the non-participants they introduced to the study were likely to be of a similar age or older. Respondents were based in a range of locations both urban and rural in England, Wales and Northern Ireland; in this phase of the research, it proved impossible to involve any older people living in Scotland in spite of concerted efforts to encourage various groups to take

Table 4.1 Age and gender of the questionnaire respondents (No.)

Age (years)	Involved in organized learning		Not involved in organized learning	
	Male	Female	Male	Female
50–54	–	–	–	2
55–59	–	2	–	–
60–64	–	5	2	2
65–69	4	5	–	2
70–74	6	5	5	6
75–79	2	1	3	4
80 or over	1	4	6	7
Total	13	22	16	23

Note: An additional three participant respondents did not indicate their ages.

part. All the respondents described themselves as white with one being of European origin; two other respondents indicated that they had been born outside the UK but had moved here before the age of four. This time it proved impossible to recruit any ethnic minority respondents in spite of considerable effort on our part.

Of all the respondents, 20 per cent classified their father's main occupation as professional and 13 per cent as semi-professional. Forty-five per cent described their father's occupation as skilled manual with a further 9 per cent being semi-skilled or unskilled manual (13 per cent). There were no significant differences between those people currently involved formally in learning and those not so involved and their fathers' main occupations. Just under half of all the respondents (47 per cent) also recalled their mothers undertaking some kind of paid work while they were children although they stressed that this was fitted in around raising a family rather than being indicative of a career. Almost 79 per cent of all respondents described their childhood home(s) as being privately owned or privately rented. Fifteen per cent had families who had been council tenants, with the remainder living in other circumstances. These figures probably reflect the very different housing realities of the period in which many of the respondents would have grown up.

Learning during childhood and early adulthood

Two of the participants and three of the non-participants claimed to have completed their full-time education before their fourteenth birthday. As the official school leaving age was raised to 14 in 1918 through the Fisher Education Act, the circumstances in which this could have happened were not explained. However, 32 per cent of the participants reported that they had acquired a school leaving qualification, 18 per cent had completed their full-time education between ages 16 and 18, and 16 per cent had undertaken some form of higher education. Fourteen per cent of the non-participants also reported having acquired a leaving certificate although 52 per cent had not done so. Four of them had completed their education between 16 and 18 and six had been over 18. The remainder did not indicate. A higher proportion of the participants (32 per cent) than non-participants (26 per cent) had also received some form of scholarship for at least part of their compulsory education. Under the terms of the 1902 Balfour Education Act that gave control of education to county councils and witnessed the setting up of local education authorities, this would have enabled 'bright' elementary pupils to attend a grammar school.

A higher proportion of the participants also had siblings who had continued in education beyond compulsory school leaving age or had studied at college level. Eighteen per cent of all respondents also reported that they had at least one sibling who had attended a university, with no significant differences between participants and non-participants. However, in view of the many changes that have taken place over the years in the organization of compulsory, post-compulsory and higher education, some of the respondents may not have easily discriminated between different types of educational institutions or have been well informed about the type of study their siblings undertook.

Many of the focus group members had talked about the importance of library membership during childhood. Overall, over two-thirds of these respondents (68 per cent) recalled being members of a library with a higher proportion of the participants than the non-participants (76 per cent as compared with 58 per cent). Participants were also slightly more likely than non-participants to rate library membership as very important in terms of their childhood learning; but, of course, this can only be a general impression as the nature of the impact of library membership on learning was not explored further at individual level.

Initially, evidence from these small samples seems to indicate that those currently participating in formally organized learning came from families with slightly higher levels of educational attainment in childhood and early adulthood than non-participants, in spite of similarities in fathers' occupational status. They appear to have been slightly more likely to have received some form of support for their education and more likely to be in possession of a qualification. We shall return to these findings later.

Adult lives: working life

Ninety-five per cent of all the respondents had married at some point in their adult lives. When asked about their main occupation during adulthood, perhaps surprisingly, almost equal proportions of participants and non-participants claimed to have been employed in professional occupations (32 and 31 per cent respectively). However, far more of the participants described their main occupation as semi-professional (37 per cent) or skilled manual (24 per cent) compared with the non-participants (19 per cent and 12 per cent). In addition, 14 per cent of the female non-participants categorized their main occupation as 'housewife and mother' or 'housewife' (5 per cent). In view of the number of female non-participants whom we knew to be over 80 years of age, it is likely that this is a reflection of a time when expectations of women's roles were rather different in that a woman was not generally expected to have a job especially if raising a family. None of the participant women saw herself as having been in this category, suggesting that, as they were somewhat younger, more of them had had jobs than their non-participant counterparts. However, it does raise the question of whether women's experience of working life is a factor in encouraging them to engage with formal educational activity in later life.

It was also noted that participants were more likely than non-participants to have had spouses or partners in professional or semi-professional occupations (60 per cent compared with 39 per cent). Again, this may be a reflection of traditional roles. Participants also reported a higher proportion of children in professional occupations although the differences were much less marked (61 per cent as opposed to 54 per cent), perhaps a demonstration of the broadening of opportunities for younger age groups. Again, it is worth considering how far children's educational attainment and occupational success influence the likelihood of parents remaining or becoming engaged with learning in later life. Evidence from an early study of older Open University graduates (over 60 years of age) showed that awareness of children or other relatives already engaged in study often acted as a motivational spur and was also seen as a major source of encouragement to older people who decided to study with the Open University (Kelly 1992).

Although no direct questions were asked about income, if home ownership is taken as a measure of financial status then participants appeared to have been more favourably placed in that nearly 90 per cent of them had owned their own homes compared with 69 per cent of non-participants; 5 per cent had lived in social housing compared with 19 per cent of the non-participants. Slightly more of the latter had rented privately or lived in other circumstances. However, overall all the respondents appeared to have lived in generally better material circumstances than had been the case during childhood. They were not asked whether they still lived at the same address in retirement but it may have been the case that some had downsized or moved to be nearer to children or indeed, moved in with children or other relatives later on in life. We were certainly aware that the respondents from Northern Ireland now lived in a sheltered housing complex or 'fold' although no one actually drew attention to any changes in their circumstances.

Learning during working life

The questions in this section required respondents to think back over their adult lives prior to retirement and to recall what kinds of learning they did, if any. Overall, 92 per cent of the participants reported engagement in some kind of learning activity compared to 76 per cent of non-participants. When this was examined in more depth, it became apparent that for both groups, of those who had been in the labour market, work-related training and continuing professional development were the main ways in which respondents had taken part in learning activity, with 10 per cent gaining vocational qualifications. Over a third of all respondents also commented that they had gained qualifications in order to keep abreast of changes in their job. Day release and attendance at evening classes at a technical college or college of further education were mainly mentioned as the ways in which these qualifications had been obtained, doubtless reflecting the main educational options available at the time, especially for men, although some of the female respondents had also studied in this way.

Respondents were also asked about any other learning they might have undertaken. This would include any learning they had carried out alone (self-directed learning), a short interest course or learning related to sport or leisure tuition. Fifty-four per cent of participants recalled some of this kind of learning compared with 44 per cent of non-participants, although 8 per cent and 3 per cent respectively (mainly women) said that all their learning during working age had been of this nature. Conversely, it was interesting that, compared with just under a quarter of participants, 41 per cent of non-participants said that they had never taken part in any learning for leisure or pleasure during working life although it may be that they had forgotten or did not consider some forms of activity in which they may have been involved as learning. Again a higher number of participants (92 per cent) were members of a library during this time and 45 per cent rated this as very important compared with the 78 per cent of non-participants who had also been library members but did not rate its importance so highly. Overall, these findings raise the question of how far educational experiences during working life – whether learning for work and/or for leisure-related purposes – may impact on learning decisions and choices in later life. Certainly, reading appears to have been an important facet of life for many of our respondents.

Adult life: post-work

Respondents were asked about their current circumstances in some detail at this point in the questionnaire. It appeared that a higher proportion of participants (63 per cent) than non-participants (52 per cent) were still married or had remarried, with a higher percentage of the latter being widowed (38 per cent as opposed to 29 per cent) or single (5 per cent against 3 per cent). The remainder did not indicate their marital status. The higher proportion of widowed people among the non-participants may, of course, be a reflection of the fact that non-participants were generally older. The divorce rate was comparable between the two groups at around 5 per cent. This finding raises the issue of how far having a presumably supportive partner can be a factor in encouraging later life learning or whether it is being alone that motivates people to seek out learning opportunities. Either factor may play a part depending on individual circumstances and disposition.

Respondents were also asked about the circumstances surrounding their retirement and becoming post-work in the sense that we had defined it. Although 5 per cent of all respondents were still undertaking some part-time or casual form of paid work, around 80 per cent of the non-participants who had been in the labour market had retired in what they considered to be generally favourable circumstances (normal retirement

age, self-planned early retirement or an acceptable offer of early retirement) compared to only 64 per cent of the participants. Retirement due
to redundancy or ill-health accounted for only 11 per cent of the other
non-participants compared with 25 per cent of the participants, although
other non-participants were more likely to have retired because of caring
responsibilities. Other respondents, mainly women, had not retired from
work in the traditional sense as they were already outside the labour
market but some had experienced a change in domestic circumstances.
Does participation in formally organized learning in some way come to
represent a partial substitute for paid work and/or to offer a new structure
to the week? To what extent might retirement circumstances considered
adverse by the retired person be a motivational factor in the decision to
become engaged in or to continue learning post-work? We hoped to begin
to explore these questions further in the next stage of the research.

Actual length of time spent post-work also appears to be a factor as
the majority of non-participants (73 per cent) had been retired for over
ten years as opposed to 36 per cent of participants, doubtless reflecting
their older ages. However, it was also noted that the percentage of non-
participants who had retired within the last three years was slightly higher
(14 per cent) than for the participants (8 per cent). How far does stage of
retirement have a bearing on learning choices and activity post-work? The
evidence from these small samples suggests that between three and ten
years following retirement is the optimal period for taking part in learning
activity. It may be that the initial years of retirement offer the chance to
'wind down' from work and become accustomed to one's new status after
which people begin to seek out more fulfilling ways of structuring their
lives.

Respondents were also asked about other aspects of their current lives.
Levels of caring responsibilities now appeared to be similar in both groups;
and very small numbers of both participants and non-participants were
receiving support because of physical disability, mental ill-health or problems associated with advancing age. This support was provided by spouses,
by other family members and by social services. Only eight respondents in
total said they were themselves giving support to children or grandchildren
but this excluded occasional childcare or babysitting duties which many of
the other respondents mentioned undertaking.

Seventy-one per cent of all respondents had held a driving licence at
some stage of their lives. However, only 53 per cent of non-participants still
drove a car compared with 78 per cent of participants, again probably a
reflection of their ages. In addition, only 5 per cent of participants reported
having a physical disability that would prevent them using public transport
compared to 18 per cent of the non-participants. Access to free or sub-
sidized transport appeared to be comparable between the two groups but
it does seem, as has been consistently shown in a range of other studies
over the years, that access to a car and ease of use of public transport can

help to facilitate participation in a range of learning and social activities whilst lack of it often presents a formidable barrier. In fact, free bus travel for everyone over 60 years of age is now available in all four UK countries but, whilst this may be a major bonus for those in urban areas, there are obviously still issues for older people in rural locations where public transport may be very infrequent or virtually non-existent.

As seen in earlier periods of life, membership of a library continued to be higher post-work for participants than for non-participants (71 per cent against 62 per cent) and the importance of membership was still rated more highly by the participants. However, although membership for both groups was highest during the working life period of adulthood, it appears that the local library still played quite a large part in the lives of the majority of both participants and non-participants. It was not clear whether they used the library just for borrowing books or for reference purposes or whether they also took advantage of the other services many libraries now offer, including borrowing films and musical recordings and access to the internet and to email.

Learning post-work

In this section of the questionnaire we asked some quite complex questions about respondents' current involvement in learning. In particular, we differentiated between formally organized learning activity and informal learning activity. We defined the latter to include 'any activity that *you* do, *planned* or *unplanned*, that *you* consider to involve some form of learning, but which is *not* formally organized or directed by anyone else'. We also asked about any past learning since retirement and any plans for the future. Results are shown in Tables 4.2 and 4.3.

Of the participants, it was noted that a high proportion were planning to continue learning formally and a similar proportion (though not necessarily the same people) said they were also learning informally. Of the small number who did not perceive themselves to be undertaking any informal learning at the moment, more than half said they had nevertheless done so

Table 4.2 Participants' learning activities (number of mentions)

Currently involved in organized learning	38
Plan to continue	25
Also currently learning informally	25
Not currently learning informally	10
Have done so since retirement	6
Planning some informal learning for the future	5
No information given	3

Table 4.3 Non-participants' learning activities (number of mentions)

Have participated in formal learning since retirement	9
May do so in future	7
Currently learning informally	13
Not currently learning informally but have done some informal learning since retirement	3
Planning some informal learning for the future	3
No learning since retirement	14
No information given	2

since retirement and five had some idea of the kind of informal learning they might want to do in future.

Interestingly, those whom we had described as non-participants revealed that this was not necessarily an appropriate designation. Although 14 of the 37 people who replied to our questions in this section reported that they had not undertaken any kind of learning since retirement, nine had themselves been involved in formally organized learning at some point and seven (again, not necessarily the same people) indicated that they had given some thought to doing so in future. Thirteen people (including eight of those who had participated formally in the past) were currently involved in informal learning and three had definite plans for some future informal learning. Furthermore, we observed that those who reported no learning since retirement tended to be at the older end of the age range so it may be that they had simply forgotten about any earlier involvement. We also allowed for the fact that, in all cases, having to bear in mind our definitions of formally organized and informal learning while completing the question-naire may have proved difficult, and we hoped that subsequent questions and the face-to-face interviews would aid clarification for all respondents.

Participants were asked to categorize the type of formal learning in which they were currently involved together with any they had already done since retirement and any formal learning intentions for the future (Table 4.4). It can be seen that learning to use a computer was currently the most popular subject of formal study and was also most often cited as the topic people were planning to learn about in future. However, in the past, arts and crafts and leisure or fitness had been the main focus of par-ticipants' activities so this development may well demonstrate how these older people were keen to keep abreast of information technology and to exploit its potential. Learning a language and travel in the sense of prepa-ration to visit other countries by learning about them in advance was also consistently cited as a continuing interest, with good intentions about undertaking leisure and fitness-related learning also featuring. By way of contrast, the subjects studied by the small number of non-participants who said they had undertaken formally organized learning in the past were

Table 4.4 Classification of participants' current formally organized learning
            activity (number of mentions)

Computing	21
Arts and crafts	13
Leisure or fitness	13
Academic related subject (no qualification or exams)	10
Languages or travel	8
Academic-related subject leading to a qualification	7
Music	5
Other	4

much more evenly spread across the subject areas, including music; three people had also achieved academic qualifications. However, any future formal learning being considered was also more likely to be specifically related to arts and crafts and also to language learning and travel.

Finally in this section, we noted that just under half of the formally organized learning currently being undertaken took place in a community centre. Nine people, mainly involved with U3A, were learning in someone's home and six in a university (respondents may have included study with the Open University or with U3A as well as that undertaken in a traditional institute of higher education). However, other learning environments included sports and leisure facilities, museums and art galleries, a library, an adult education college, a further education college, a school, sheltered accommodation, Age Concern premises and a hospice. Some participants were learning at more than one site. It appears that these older people were generally quite flexible in where they were prepared to learn and did not necessarily expect the venue to be an educational institution. In fact, educators of adults have long stressed the desirability of local and more informal learning environments, and the availability of these appears to have been a factor in facilitating these older learners' attendance.

We also asked respondents to indicate from a range of possible factors, drawn from the focus group discussions, why they took up organized learning activity, although we were aware that questioning people retrospectively about their motivation to join a course or class can be fraught with difficulties. For example, reviewing a range of approaches, Withnall and Percy wondered whether studies that examine adults' motivation for participation in learning are 'doing no more than recounting people's post-hoc rationalizations' (1994: 49), whilst Ahl (2006) has argued forcibly that the concept of motivation should be seen as a euphemism for direction and control rather than a particular disposition residing within the individual. In devising our list of factors we hoped to help our respondents to reflect upon, and to make some sense of their decisions, rather than appearing to

Table 4.5 Participants' reasons for engaging in formally organized learning activity (number of mentions)

Keep mind active	32
Desire to learn	31
Broaden horizons	22
Enjoyment	20
Meet new people	20
Make friends	16
Wanted a challenge	14
Relaxation	12
Retirement	10
Keep body active	10

stigmatize anyone for apparent lack of participation. Participants' responses are summarized in Table 4.5.

It was noticeable that, for almost all the participants, the main reasons for joining a class or course tended to cluster around definite intentions to learn, to ensure the maintenance of an active mind and to broaden their horizons, with more social reasons appearing to be secondary. However, 'enjoyment' featured in almost half of the participants' responses and many of them actually indicated a wide range of motivations in addition to keeping an active mind, especially the chance to meet new people and make friends. Less important reasons ticked fewer than four times included 'to fill in time', 'widow(er)hood' and 'a change in caring responsibilities'. It was interesting to note that, asked the same question, the small number of non-participants who had taken part in formal learning in the past indicated that the 'desire to learn', 'to keep an active mind' and 'to broaden horizons' had also been their main reasons. They were less likely to ascribe their decision to the other possible factors, suggesting that they had decided to follow up an interest at a specific time when they perceived an appropriate opportunity to be available.

We asked participants to indicate what they saw personally as the benefits of participation in formally organized learning activity, again from a list of factors drawn from the focus group discussions. Results are shown in Table 4.6. Certainly, their desire to learn appears to have been fulfilled since all those who responded in this section reported that new knowledge had been the main outcome, accompanied for almost all by enjoyment and a sense of self-satisfaction. Those who had hoped to make friends also seem to have largely fulfilled this aim and a large proportion reported a renewed interest in life, especially those who were living alone. Interestingly, the non-participants who had taken part in the past recorded self-satisfaction and friendship as the main outcomes they recalled from their previous

Table 4.6 What participants got from engaging in formally organized
learning activity (number of mentions)

Knowledge	32
Enjoyment	25
Self-satisfaction	23
Friendship	23
Interest in life	21
Increased awareness	14
Relaxation	11
Feeling included	11

activity, with acquisition of knowledge some way behind. However, this may reflect the kinds of learning in which they had participated, which, as previously noted, appear to have included a broader range of activities, some resulting in a qualification, others with a more practical focus. It may be that they had seen learning as something of a challenge and that making new friends had been an additional unanticipated outcome.

We also asked the non-participants to indicate any reasons why they were not currently taking part in formal learning. Reasons may be complex and fewer than half these respondents attempted a response. The main reason, selected nine times, was 'don't have time because of other activities' although 'getting there is too difficult' also featured five times. Lack of time was also the main reason given for non-participation in informal learning. This suggests that, if these respondents are typical, older people, whether or not they see themselves as learners, are generally leading busy and active lives in which they are involved with a whole range of activities. Some may also already have a number of regular commitments whatever their chronological age.

It has already been seen that a majority of participants also reported that they were learning informally. Asked what form this learning took, getting to grips with computers was again named as the main activity with 12 responses; this may have been self-teaching, the result of instruction from a family member, or could have taken the form of practice learning at home to consolidate what was being formally taught in a course or class. Learning related to arts and crafts was practised by 11 people and was also most likely to be a past interest and one that participants intended to continue or take up in future along with a desire to learn a language or expand travel knowledge. Eleven people also reported that they were engaged in academic study (not leading to a qualification) mostly related to extra study as a result of U3A membership; one woman ascribed the considerable amount of non-fiction reading she did to this category. Other interests, not categorized, related to gardening, reading about theology and learning from television programmes.

Questions about reasons for engaging with informal learning once again revealed that a desire to learn and to keep an active mind were the main motivational factors, although a sense of enjoyment also featured as did the need for relaxation. Asked about the perceived outcomes of informal learning, 21 participants responded; other participants may have found that this question did not lend itself to any easy answers. Responses are shown in Table 4.7. Once again, knowledge and enjoyment were seen as the main outcomes. However, it appears that informal learning was also helping these participants maintain an interest in life in general and to increase their awareness (although we did not explore what they meant by this at an individual level) as well as making a contribution to their sense of self-satisfaction. The overall impression is that complementing formal learning with informally based activities, even if these are a component of more formal activity, can have positive and enjoyable outcomes for these older people's lives. Most of the informal learning undertaken was described as taking place in the home or garden, further suggesting that one of its features is its flexibility in that learners can fit it in around their lifestyles without any need to travel; but museums and galleries were also acknowledged as sites of informal learning for five participants who enjoyed regular visits. We also asked non-participants about any informal learning with which they might be engaged. As seen above, 13 reported that they were currently involved in some kind of informal learning, including eight of those who had done some formal learning since retirement; and three had considered undertaking some informal learning in future. There were four mentions of some current academic study not leading to a qualification, but arts and crafts were most likely to be the learning focus of this group both past and present and for the future. Those who had done some formal learning in the past also mentioned languages or travel and learning through listening to music as enduring activities. There was far less overall interest in learning about computers. As with the participants, home and garden were the main sites for informal learning. Again, it may

Table 4.7 What participants got from engaging in informally organized learning activity (number of mentions)

Knowledge	19
Enjoyment	18
Interest in life	16
Increased awareness	15
Self-satisfaction	14
Friendship	10
Relaxation	9
Health benefits	7

be the fact that these respondents were generally older than the participants that may account for their preference for the kinds of unstructured
informal learning that they could largely undertake at home, especially as
'enjoyment' and 'self satisfaction' were seen as the main outcomes. Their
apparent lack of interest in computers may have been because they did not
see any need to engage with them at this stage of their lives.

'Learning is . . . '

Although we had given a brief explanation of our understanding of
'formal' and 'informal' learning within the questionnaire, the sentence
completion task previously described was designed to elicit how older
people themselves interpret the concept of learning. Eighty-six per cent of
all the respondents attempted the task and their definitions were analysed
to identify any emergent key themes. Perhaps surprisingly, no particular
differences between participants and non-participants' beliefs emerged.

Learning is . . . acquiring knowledge

Over 40 per cent of the definitions provided contained an explicit reference
to gaining or increasing knowledge or developing skills.

> Learning is . . .
>
> . . . the acquisition of knowledge, skills and wisdom.
>
> . . . acquiring a new skill or knowledge.
>
> . . . gaining knowledge or skills by study or experience.
>
> . . . extending knowledge about familiar interests.

Learning is . . . about living

In the majority of cases, however, the idea of gaining knowledge and/or
skills was only part of the definition. The process of acquiring knowledge
and skills was also seen as offering opportunities to become more receptive
to new ideas, to broaden one's horizons and to generally develop the mind.
One female respondent also stressed that learning arises from within the
individual; it is something different from merely being present while someone teaches in that it involves personal growth and a sense of personal
satisfaction. In general, these respondents took a more holistic view of what
learning entails.

> Learning is . . .
>
> . . . acquiring knowledge, which adds structure to one's life. It enlarges
> one's perspective.

Also it's the gaining of new skills, which hopefully, makes you a more interesting person.

. . . about living; all activities whether domestic or leisure provide learning opportunities although we don't always realize this at the time. Confirmation comes with practical application.

. . . any activity that reveals details of anything that was previously unknown. We are learning all the time during our daily activities, out and about, even sometimes when watching TV.

. . . [something that can] happen in many ways – a dawdle in the country, a conversation with a friend. We learn every day; how to grow old, keep happy, content and help others. Life *is* learning.

Learning is . . . *successful ageing*

Perhaps because these were older people, learning was frequently described in terms of helping one to achieve what was seen as 'successful' ageing and to remain part of society. Once again, many respondents laid stress on the importance of keeping an active mind and the various benefits that they perceived would ensue, as these selected quotes demonstrate.

Learning is . . .

. . . very good for keeping an active mind which is important for the older person. It also makes you feel you are part of society and not getting left behind everyone else.

. . . about preparing the mind to accept new ideas – new concepts – and enables one to address problems at all levels. In retirement, to have a prepared mind is essential to living a full and satisfied life.

. . . giving interest to every day and also confidence in yourself. [It] leads to a happier, healthier outlook and therefore [the ability] to cope with all the extra hours to fill after retirement.

Learning is . . . *a matter of perspective*

For other respondents, learning was seen as a way of maintaining a positive outlook and indeed, of expanding one's perspective on life in a constructive way. Both participants and non-participants expressed variants on this view but it tended to be the older respondents who offered thoughts along the lines of those focus group members who were living in a residential home. Some people had obviously given considerable time to thinking how best to express their thoughts on this issue and answered at length. Here we reproduce just some brief quotes that were typical of the beliefs that emerged.

Learning is . . .

. . . the opening of the mind and being receptive to different ideas . . . Learning is knowledge of what is all around oneself. It stimulates the mind to imagination and invention.

. . . a great adventure into unknown territory where you find there is still more to learn. Learning opens up new opportunities in living and is full of wonderful surprises.

Learning is . . . *understanding the modern world*

Learning was also seen as an important way of keeping up with an ever-changing world, especially through being able to understand and to use modern technology. This was certainly the case among many of the participants who had already demonstrated their enthusiasm for learning about computers. However, it also emerged here as an important facet of remaining engaged with both family and society at large.

Learning is . . .

. . . [a way of] opening up lots of other things, for example, making new friends and in my case, being able to communicate with my family in Italy and keeping up with the modern world and technology.

. . . getting to know something new about the world we live in, the people in that world, or skills that enable us to live and grow and be happy.

. . . an ongoing engine through life helping us all to cope with an ever-changing world . . . widening our horizons from youth to maturity.

Learning is . . . *good for your health*

Finally, learning was described by three people as a way of preventing ill-health and even as a form of therapy.

Learning is . . .

. . . one of the prime reasons for life. Without learning one becomes very stressed, agitated and depressed. Consequently, this leads to ill-health. Learning is a basic need that human beings need to survive and thrive.

. . . very important and, depending on the individual, can be very therapeutic.

. . . good therapy.

In reality, these were not absolutely discrete categories, as many of the comments overlapped. However, the broad themes identified appear to demonstrate the varied ideas different older people have about what constitutes learning. Even among some of those who were not currently engaged, there appeared to be an acknowledgement of the role that learning, in its various guises, can play in older people's lives. Certainly, further weight was lent to the emerging belief that opportunities to learn are all around and do not necessarily depend on being formally taught in a class or course.

Respondents' reflections

At the end of the questionnaire, respondents were invited to add any additional thoughts about their experiences of education or of learning at any stage. Because many of the kinds of comments made were relevant to our aim of reconsidering our model of learning across the life course as derived from the focus group discussions, we have again analysed these comments thematically this time in relation to the model, giving brief examples of the kinds of issues that were raised.

Time: experiencing disruption and change

We previously noted the way in which different aspects of time appear to be important in affecting older people's educational and learning experiences across the life course and, hence, their views about learning. Indeed, attention has more recently been drawn to the importance of different dimensions of time (and place) in understanding patterns of participation in learning opportunities (Gorard and Selwyn 2005). Here, as in the focus groups, a varied range of comments again illustrated that disruption and structural change can have a major impact on people's life experiences and, by implication, on their educational opportunities. Once again the Second World War and its aftermath was seen to have had a major impact. For example, a male respondent described how his career changed as a result of the war:

> I attained a scholarship at 14-plus to a local secondary school . . . I then had a few years in a highly successful industrial engineering firm. Then I saw in 1939 that war was imminent so I went into the aircraft business. When the war ended, I went straight into shipbuilding, which I enjoyed until compulsory retirement in 1978.

Similarly, a female respondent recounted how her career had developed, and wondered whether it might have been different had circumstances allowed. 'When I left school at 16, my first job was as a clerk . . . If my father had not been killed in the war when I was aged three, undoubtedly

I would have stayed on for further education but finances did not allow this to happen.'

To some extent, this might be also seen as a situational influence. However, a male respondent commented, as had some of the focus group participants, that his two years' National Service was a significant factor in his eventual choice of career in civilian life. There were also some comments from female respondents relating to change over time. For example: 'Having children put a stop to my career. By the time I returned to work, my skills were out of date because the office had become computerized.' In spite of this, it was possible to detect a general feeling that, as one respondent said, 'our age group always seems to muddle through', reflecting the sense of personal continuity and ability to cope with change that had also emerged in the focus group discussions.

Situational influences on access to education and learning

Rather fewer situational influences on respondents' access to education and learning were recalled, although there were some grateful memories of family encouragement and sacrifice. 'I failed my 11-plus exam and am forever grateful to my parents in that they scraped and saved to send me to grammar school. That made an enormous difference to the course of my life.' Lack of money was mentioned more than once as a lifelong barrier to better educational opportunities. However, there were adverse personal situations that had had positive outcomes. One older man wrote about how a stroke the previous year had resulted in a referral to a charitable organization where he had been enabled to take a range of courses as part of his rehabilitation and had himself become a tutor in spite of 'being not very bright and always shy' at school. After becoming a widower, another had turned to voluntary work at an Age Concern Centre where he made new friends and developed his own practical craft skills.

Institutional influences on education and learning

Many of those who reflected on their educational histories could pinpoint specific experiences in one or more of the educational institutions they had attended at some point. As in most of the focus groups, reminiscences of school days were generally favourable and teachers gratefully remembered:

> During schooling from 1935 to 1945, whilst I admit that certain items of the curriculum were not to my liking, school was a good place to acquire a wide knowledge of many subjects that were going to prove very useful in later life. Teachers appeared to be dedicated and fair, giving help where needed and administering discipline in a reasonable manner.

There were also further mentions of passing the 11-plus examination and attending a grammar school that had opened up opportunities, at least in the short term. Two people made a particular note of the educational institutions they had attended to acquire qualifications during working life, with one man commenting that his previous lack of qualifications did not hold him back in this respect; both respondents were subsequently enabled to change direction in their careers. However, there were more detailed accounts of decisions made to study for an Open University degree in later life by two people and an assessment of the difference this had made. 'I did an OU degree in my fifties. I think it changed me absolutely – one thing I learnt straight away was that there was so much I didn't know . . . It seemed to cheer me up and spur me on and gave me more confidence in the world.' Both these respondents commented on the sense of pride they had experienced on being awarded their degrees.

Individual influences

Apart from the personal stories already told, there were fewer comments regarding individual influences on learning than had emerged in the focus groups, but it was nevertheless apparent that some of the respondents had developed their own philosophies around the place of learning as a result of life experiences. As one woman who had been able to take advantage of a range of formal learning opportunities in her area put it: 'I believe that we should never stop learning and I'm glad that so much is offered to us, possibilities are endless. No one knows everything but knowledge is powerful . . . The importance of knowledge is how one uses it.' Yet another woman who was not currently learning formally wrote:

> To me, talking with people (or rather listening to people) educated or uneducated – is education. So whether get togethers are social or educational, you're still learning. It's easy for older people, especially if shy, to get into a rut and stay at home especially if not mobile. Any organization, council or voluntary, is good if well enough organized to appeal and encourage older people to have an enjoyable life.

This respondent seems to be saying that learning can happen through a range of organizations or situations and is not necessarily limited to what is offered by educational institutions, a view that many of the respondents appeared to share. She was also less condemnatory than some focus group members had been in respect of older people who did not appear to be leading particularly active lives.

Conclusion

Our findings, although based on small samples of older people, suggest that the model we developed as a result of the focus group discussions had some validity. In particular, the ongoing influence of time in its various guises intertwined with the availability of educational opportunities, institutional influences, social expectations and individual beliefs, capacity and willingness to participate in learning activities again appeared in the questionnaire responses as factors that encourage or discourage later life learning. What also emerged was that older people interpret learning in a variety of ways; non-participation in formally organized learning does not imply lack of interest in learning *per se*. With these clues as to how later life learning happens, we wanted to explore further some of these older people's beliefs about learning and, in particular, their learning experiences post-work. This is the substance of the next chapter.

Chapter 5

No limits to learning?

Introduction

In this phase of the study, the kinds of learning activities currently undertaken and identified in the questionnaire responses were explored in more depth through interviews with some of the questionnaire respondents and through the use of learning 'logs' or diaries. In particular, the emphasis was now on obtaining a fuller picture of some of the respondents' day-to-day lives post-work and further exploration of their current experiences of, and views about, learning through listening to the voices of these older people themselves. In this way, it was hoped to obtain a better understanding of the very wide contexts in which these older people were currently undertaking what they saw as learning, how it was accommodated in their daily lives and its significance to them. Accordingly, it was again equally important to obtain the views both of older people currently enrolled in a class or course and those of who were not presently participating formally but who may have seen themselves as learning in other ways.

Data collection and analysis

The methods used in this stage of the research consisted of a series of semi-structured interviews carried out by a team of seven older people themselves and the use of a learning 'log' or diary. These methods, the reasons for their selection and the issues that arose from their use are discussed in detail in the Appendix, as are the processes and implications of involving older people in interviewing their peers. However, it can be noted here that, of those who returned the questionnaire and agreed to take part further, 25 of the participants and 25 of the non-participants were randomly selected for interview. Of these, 21 participants and 14 non-participants confirmed their willingness to be interviewed; others had encountered circumstances that meant they could no longer take part or had simply changed their minds. Of the participants, 17 were women and four were men; this may reflect the longevity and greater preponderance of women in formally organized courses and classes. Of the women, six were married; four were divorced and four widowed whilst the other three had not indicated their marital status. All four men were married. However, there was a more even gender balance among the non-participants, who consisted of eight men and six women. Five of these men were married and two were widowed, one of whom was registered blind, plus one other whose marital status had not been indicated. Five of the women were married although it was interesting to note that three of them made a point of noting that their husbands were sometimes away from home for at least part of the week because they were still working in some capacity. It was apparent from information previously given in the questionnaires that the interviewees ranged in age from the late sixties, mainly female participants, to the late eighties, with the male non-participants tending to be at the upper end of the age range. Interviewees were located in a variety of different areas, both urban and rural, with three participants living in a fold in Northern Ireland and one in similar accommodation in the south of England. Two other participants were carers to another family member although they had not previously drawn much attention to this or mentioned any particular impact on their lives.

Of the 20 other questionnaire respondents who agreed to keep a learning log for two months of all the activities they undertook that they would classify as 'learning', only nine managed the task and then only for between one and two months. As discussed in the Appendix, this exercise may have proved too arduous and demanding a chore. Nevertheless, the older people who did participate in the exercise completed their diaries with care and diligence and this enabled some useful information to be extrapolated. The learning log was designed to be kept for a two-month period divided into eight or nine weekly sections (depending on the months).

Findings

The interviews

A considerable amount of qualitative data was generated through the interviews. The themes that emerged are discussed here in some detail, illustrated by direct quotes from both sets of interviewees where appropriate.

Enjoyment of life post-work

We were interested to discover what aspects of their post-work lives interviewees particularly enjoyed. A sense of freedom, mainly from the strictures imposed by paid work, and having choice about how to spend one's time emerged as the main aspects of life that both groups of interviewees chose to stress. This was sometimes illustrated at length through examples of various leisure activities that had been taken up in retirement, often in conjunction with a spouse or friend. The participant women living in a fold felt that this had added considerably to the general quality of their lives in that they always had people around them and plenty of activities on offer. Having more time to spend with the family, especially grandchildren, and with friends was also seen as an enjoyable aspect of life and was particularly valuable for those who had recently been bereaved. Although almost everyone liked the area where they lived, non-participants were more likely to mention the pleasure they obtained from their home, garden and general environment. Many of the respondents' lives seemed to be particularly full but there was also an overall appreciation of the slower pace of life that retirement offered. Others expressed their gratitude at being financially 'comfortable' in retirement, although in some cases outsiders might have been surprised by this assertion since some of the interviewees appeared to be living in reduced circumstances. One woman added that being needed and helping others was now one of the most pleasurable aspects of her life.

Issues that detracted from enjoyment of life for both groups mainly related to personal health problems or those of relatives, with one man's life having become gradually more restricted because of his wife's disability. There were also individual instances where the life-changing effects of chronic conditions such as diabetes or arthritis were described in detail; but it was the general sense of gradual age-related changes in eyesight, hearing and mobility and an awareness of growing older that were most often cited as tiresome or annoying in that they sometimes limited activities that had previously been enjoyed or made housework and shopping more difficult. Living alone and widow(er)hood were also seen as negative factors although lack of friends in the vicinity also tended to be an issue for the two people who had relocated following retirement. Only two participants mentioned financial problems but another woman also expressed more general worries about violence in society and fears for the future. However, in spite of these various concerns, there was a definite sense that any problems could be lived with and interviewees were surprisingly cheerful and positive in their outlook. Overall, there was really very little that spoilt enjoyment of life for either group, with six participants and one non-participant stressing that they were generally 'very content'.

The organization of daily life post-work

There is, of course, an already considerable and expanding literature especially within sociology, cultural and feminist studies that attempts to grapple with aspects of the social organization of everyday life and the use of time. In relation to the everyday lives of older people, the ways in which qualitative methods have been used to record various aspects have also been discussed (Bytheway 2003). Here all the interviewees spoke at length about features of their daily lives, giving a variety of examples of the range of activities and interests in which they were involved, and reflected on the ways in which their lives were organized to accommodate them. In this respect, it was noticeable that some of the married interviewees found it difficult to focus solely on themselves and included their spouses in their responses to illustrate that they did most things together or, in choosing and arranging their own activities, took the spouse's commitments and interests into account. In some cases, a consequence of retirement appeared to have been a recognition that a fair use of time needed to be carefully negotiated and domestic chores sometimes traded to enable both partners to follow up their individual interests as well as the activities that they enjoyed as a couple.

Marital status did not seem to influence whether or not interviewees adhered to a strict daily or weekly routine although it was noticeable that the non-participant men were more likely than others to describe a more structured day. Those in this category who were married tended to fit in with what their wives were doing or looked forward to regular visits from family members that spouses had organized for particular days of the week; or they structured their day around specific regular commitments such as 'taking the dog for a walk'. This was greatly valued as a way of getting regular exercise and a chance to chat to people encountered en route and was frequently cited as an important feature of pet owners' daily lives. For another man, having diabetes meant that the structure of his family's day was dictated largely by the timing of his insulin injections and need for regular mealtimes, a routine that he accepted philosophically, stressing that it did not prevent him from undertaking regular activity both on his own and with his wife.

> I go into the village and get my papers and have a chat. I like a lunch at the proper time. The wife always cooks a proper meal. I stay in and do a few jobs in the shed and read and do some crosswords. Fridays is shopping with the wife. Saturday I go to watch rugby and I go by myself and meet some old school friends . . . There's a pensioners' club in the village and we tried it but we'd rather go for a walk instead of playing bingo. Perhaps later on when we're less mobile. We do belong to a Retirement Fellowship run by the NHS which I am chairman of. I go to a diabetic clinic. Sometimes we go to a concert because we do like music and we like singing very much.

The two widowed men who were non-participants both mentioned Sunday as an important day in the week when they saw relatives, but both admitted to otherwise spending a lot of time alone. However, one who was now registered blind wanted to talk about two other particularly pleasurable interludes in his week.

> There is an old man here in the building and he's 84 but he's really more active than me and we go down to the park beside us and we

> throw crumbs and crusts to the birds. We don't go very far now. We used to go round the lake but now we go as far as the bridge and back again. I frequent the library a good deal now that I can't read. I get the audio books. Every time I go there she [the library assistant] has half a dozen picked out for me. Everybody knows me. I 'read' everything.

The women interviewees in both categories were more likely to talk about having a regular weekly, rather than daily routine although they mostly stressed that this was flexible and that they were adaptable 'when things crop up'. It was noticeable that all the women participants were involved in a range of other activities sometimes related to their church, religious group or synagogue or in voluntary work in addition to the courses or classes that they attended. These women tended to be 'out every day' and, although they did receive some visits from family and friends, they generally felt they had very little time to entertain at home. One married woman participant offered a general overview of her life that included some activities she undertook alone whilst others also involved her husband.

> I like to go to the shops every day and I do like to play bridge once a week. I do have lots of friends who we visit for coffee and tea and dinner in the evening. I like to watch television, documentaries and *Who Wants to Be a Millionaire?* We see the family regularly and do a lot of gardening in the summer time. We enjoy travel. We watch sport. We are bowlers and that is a sport we actually participate in – we belong to a club. We walk a lot and feel that lots of exercise has to be taken regularly. We walk into town. We wander round the shops and have coffee out. We belong to the National Trust.

One widow whose life also appeared to be particularly full explained that 'I am about more than I am at home. I do try to do a certain amount of gardening most days but I would expect to be socially active at least five out of seven days. I would also expect to see friends at lectures I attend.' Similarly, a divorced participant who was attending a computer course described some typical activities in her week.

> I get up quite early. I am up and showered by quarter to seven. I do an aerobics tape every weekday except Thursday when I go swimming at the crack of dawn. After the aerobics and swimming the days will differ. I visit friends regularly. I garden. I like embroidery. Occasionally, I will do some housework. I do enough to keep it neat . . . I go to computers twice a week. I usually try to do a walk as well if I have enough time during the day . . . If I'm going to visit art galleries or anything cultural then I like to do it with somebody.

Unlike the men, non-participant married females also spent considerable time out of the house and were also often involved in voluntary activities as well as having days out with friends or grandchildren. However, two who had recently moved house mentioned that they were currently occupied with housework, gardening, decorating and unpacking especially where husbands were regularly absent for some days in the week. One of these women, now living in a remote part of Wales, admitted that most of her time was currently spent in the village with only a weekly shopping trip to the nearest town. She commented as follows.

> Well, we don't really know anybody here. On a daily basis we don't have any visitors. At the moment life is very solitary. The nearest town is about 25 minutes by car on very narrow roads so it's not very accessible. There is a local bus service. People in the village are very friendly but it's winter and we haven't got past the initial 'hello, we've just moved here.'

This respondent was nevertheless delighted with the beauty of the surroundings in which she was now living, stressing that she had no regrets about moving. She was very confident that her life would greatly improve once they were settled and got to know more people in the area so that a new routine would emerge and she would be ready to consider new activities.

Learning in a formal context

Participants talked at considerable length about the formally organized learning activities in which they were currently involved. In most cases, the learning described involved some kind of course or class for which fees were payable, but these varied enormously according to the organization running the class, the type of learning undertaken and its duration. Some of the learning described took place within a community or worship setting and was very low cost or free. Participants were also asked to comment on their experiences of the learning they were currently undertaking so that, overall, a number of different themes emerged.

Firstly, it quickly became apparent that many participants saw the learning in which they were currently involved and which they chose to discuss with the interviewer, along a continuum, a perception that had begun to emerge in their questionnaire responses. Although they may have taken up new interests in retirement, this was part of their ongoing identity as lifelong learners. None of the participants envisaged a time when they would not be learning, whilst acknowledging that the ways in which they learnt might need to change in future. For example, one married woman who was now involved in a range of craft activities within a small group at a community centre recounted how she had 'been learning all my life', having become an adult learner as a young mother with encouragement from a neighbour. She described the courses she had undertaken over the years ranging from keep fit and swimming to a City and Guilds teaching qualification and including an Access course that would have enabled her to study for a degree had it not been for financial restrictions. She had also become proficient in floral art and this had enabled her to earn a very small amount of money from home. Similarly, another woman talked about her current word-processing course and the poetry workshops in which she was involved as well as a two-year art appreciation course on which she had enrolled. However, she also recalled a range of other courses she had completed earlier in life including 'a couple of summer courses in Cambridge' and a photography course as well as a previous attempt to learn Greek in a local adult education centre. This reminded her of having also learnt to speak some Turkish as a young adult some fifty years ago. Looking to the future, she envisaged herself 'switching to courses over the internet' if 'something got in the way of going to organized learning'.

One of the men described in detail how his purchase of a simple camera from Woolworth's in 1949 had inspired his lifelong interest in photography and in learning generally so that he always made it his business to 'find out how best to do it' when a new challenge came along in life. Since retiring, he had taken up country and western dancing with his wife and had subsequently realized that he needed to get fitter. There were several other examples of these serial learners where one activity had sparked off interest in another, although a minority of interviewees had only taken up their current interests just before or after retirement, frequently to accompany a spouse or at the suggestion of a relative or friend.

Secondly, issues about finding a course at a suitable level and in an acceptable location also emerged. One married female interviewee who appeared to be a very active and enthusiastic learner admitted that she had 'always wanted to learn Spanish' and had tried 'a couple of times to get myself into a class or group where there was the teaching and support to really make me do it'. She had already undertaken an intensive summer course run by her nearest university followed by holidays in Spain and Peru and then decided that she 'must get back to it'. However, her efforts to find a suitable class had not been easy. As she explained:

> I went to the [local further education] college but both courses that were open were focused on what the college called 'progress'. They were sort of aimed at GCSE, which is not what I wanted to do. I was conscious that the beginners' class were going round reciting pronouns, which I didn't want to do. The advanced class were just more advanced than I was. I recognized that I was going to have to work very hard to catch up with them . . . and I couldn't commit myself to that much work.

This interviewee had since come across a conversational Spanish class attended by friends and, although she had now chosen to learn on her own through a Beginners' Spanish course on DVD, she commented on what she perceived to be the differences between the two types of class:

> Theirs was much more conversational . . . They do have a book to work from but it's not a sacred text, they just look to see how to learn something. That would suit me much better and that is probably the way most older people would like to learn. Progress in the sense that it is marked by an examiner is not what I'm after.

Problems with learning a language were similarly highlighted by another married woman who was also attending a local college with her husband. Noting that 'we enjoy languages because we like to travel', she was also currently learning Spanish but had been less successful with a Leisure French course that they had both abandoned because 'it was getting a little too technical for us'. She had also opted for a conversation class instead. She added: 'When you are in a class as a rule you go at the slowest pace but when you have a class of people who are quite good, the teacher can respond more to them than to the slow ones.' Pace appeared to be a problem in other learning situations. As an example, another married woman participant living in the north-west of England, whilst speaking at length and with considerable enthusiasm about her current activity, felt it important to describe a difficulty she had encountered:

> I am actually learning to ski. We have a ski class on a Monday morning. I have learnt something and I can actually put it into practice when I get on to snow, but just the effort of learning something physical is quite difficult for me as I can only learn one thing at a time. If I don't get enough practice doing just that one thing, the class has moved on to doing something else and I can't remember which thing I'm supposed to be doing so it's actually quite a challenge, a physical challenge.

Similarly, a woman who had been attending a computer class at a further education college remarked on the difficulties experienced in learning that she had encountered within a mixed-age class advertised as being for beginners:

> There were 25 to 30 in a class and only one tutor. Everyone else at that time except me had knowledge of computers so I couldn't keep up. It wasn't the college's fault because the other people in the class had told the college that they were the same as me, a complete beginner. I was disappointed.

This participant had subsequently gone on to complete a course specifically for older people at a community centre that had been much more successful. She felt strongly that colleges should make sure that courses advertised as being for complete beginners did really admit only those with no prior knowledge whatsoever although it may be difficult to establish this with complete certainty.

Commenting that 'I don't want to do exams now', a third married woman described the watercolour painting class she attended at a local community college in addition to a French group and book club organized through her local U3A. All these activities also entailed some additional home preparation but she commented enthusiastically on how learning about painting techniques had made her 'so much more aware of places and styles'. She had been able to exhibit and sell some of her work that then paid for her art materials. Describing her art teacher as 'very talented', she nevertheless expressed some concerns:

> They seem to be trying to cut adult education unless it is self-financing and this could make life very difficult for older people. It's to do with the local education person who doesn't like education for older people. There's always a lot of talk as to whether we shall continue. I only pay half because of being retired and there's always the threat that you'll have to pay the full amount.

We will comment on issues of cost later on, but this interviewee proved to be sadly prophetic. Because she was based in a rural part of Wales, she also expressed concerns about the rising cost of petrol since she had to travel to her chosen activities by car. Although travel to classes or courses did not appear to pose many problems for other participants, some interviewees did comment that they had chosen their courses for ease of access or because of the availability of a lift for reaching upper floors at the venue. The need to take these factors into account may have originally restricted their choice of activities. One woman who was very involved with a number of different courses would have liked to change the timing of her word-processing course held in the evening at a further education college in that she found three hours too long and had encountered difficulties over fitting in her evening meal. Having a hearing problem meant that she also sometimes had problems differentiating sounds in the classroom. However, on balance, she felt that the reasonable cost of the course and the convenience of the venue outweighed these other difficulties.

A male interviewee who had been attending a language course held in an old school building had been put off by the general lack of facilities and the fact that classrooms had to be continually rearranged and furniture moved round before teaching could begin. Another woman who had recently attended a City and Guilds photography course that she nevertheless 'thoroughly enjoyed' also commented that 'there were never enough enlargers to go round and we were always queuing up'.

These brief comments suggest that older students may weigh up perceived difficulties in the learning environment and in the facilities on offer but are prepared to make a trade-off if a course suits them in other ways. However, like all adult learners, older people should expect to be provided with suitably comfortable surroundings and appropriate facilities whatever the setting.

Thirdly, as already seen, almost all the interviewees were taking part in more than one type of formally organized learning or had moved on to a new activity at some point since retirement. The woman who was learning to ski had recently discovered her course through an advertisement in the local paper asking for people who might be interested in having a dry ski slope club in the town and had joined with her husband. Apart from improving their own abilities, she stressed how they both derived considerable satisfaction from 'watching other people learn' and seeing 'families doing things together' and had built up a good social life with the friends they had made at the club. In addition, this woman noted that she also attended a weekly U3A computer class and walking group that included 'a sociable lunch' as well as three different book clubs, although these met less frequently.

This pattern was apparent in several other interviewees' accounts of their involvement in different types of organized learning. One of the men explained that he had 'done woodwork for about five years' after he first retired at the suggestion of his wife who was 'doing floristry' but he was now enrolled on a computer course with an excellent tutor. Another man living in London spoke enthusiastically about the range of U3A classes he had tried that had included history of science, European history and various lectures as well as a new economics course. He had also been away on U3A organized holidays with his wife and had visited gardens that he would not have otherwise seen. Remarking that 'we could spend every day at the U3A if we wanted to', this man also kept up interests in the commercial property world as well as being involved with community activities through his synagogue. Similarly, a woman living in a fold described her participation in the learning programme provided there that consisted of 'just general subjects' and a computer class although she also studied music through the U3A and attended the local university for occasional lectures as well as enjoying church-based learning activities.

Learning informally

Following revelations about the extent of informal learning activity that had been uncovered in the questionnaire responses, all the interviewees elaborated further on the kinds of informal learning in which they were involved according to their own perceptions of what such learning entails.

As already seen, older people are attracted to a wide variety of activities, although those who also participated in formal courses or classes tended to have informal learning interests that related either to these or to what they saw as hobbies. For the women, these were often related to reading, with magazines, detective fiction, biographies and history as well as popular science being particularly enjoyed. A majority now also recalled that they tried completing crosswords on a regular basis and improving computer skills. Some also enjoyed gardening and visiting National Trust properties or rambling with a group. Most of the women were avid newspaper readers and enjoyed radio and television, although they generally stressed that they were highly selective about what they watched. One woman who was already busily engaged in a range of courses and classes also described how a particularly interesting television programme might 'set me off on a trail' that frequently led her to follow new lines of enquiry on her own. The male participants responded in similar ways although they were more likely to be using computers to follow up their interests or, indeed, teaching themselves to use different computer programmes. As an afterthought, a woman who was also a carer for her disabled son added that she had also learnt from meeting other carers a considerable amount about his condition and how best to manage it.

Since completing the questionnaire, a widower whom we had designated a non-participant had ventured to join a woodworking group and a beginners' computer course at a local social centre so that he had now become a participant. However, he and all but one of the non-participants were also able to discuss a whole range of ways in which they considered they were learning informally, ranging from improving photography techniques to interviewing people for an oral history project in the nearby village. In addition, two men had taken courses in the past and one had considered joining a class but had not done so. A further male interviewee with an interest in amateur radio thought he might do so in future but any course would 'have to involve conversing with other people'. However, the general feeling among the male non-participants was that they were 'too old' or that there was really now 'no need' to join a course as informal learning meant 'you can go at your own pace'. Just one forcibly expressed a different view:

> I know all I want to learn. I learnt things while I was actually working. When I retired I saw these learning activities and a lot of old people going for education. I think that's for people's own egos. I think people should learn practical skills like mending fuses or mending washers . . . I don't like the word learning. For information, yes – say about animals and birds in documentaries – but I wouldn't want anyone to teach me anything. I would only be interested in being in a group so I could talk.

Nevertheless, after some prompting, this interviewee started to talk about the 'trial and error learning' he had undertaken in the garden where he apparently spent a good deal of time. He saw gardening mainly as a very creative activity but went on to reflect further about this:

> To have a packet of seeds and watch them come to fruition – you learn from that. It's getting new information and it keeps your mind active. It's just something I'm doing, it's not learning. I don't have to sit an exam or anything . . . learning is purely incidental. I don't see why anyone should want to learn anything after they've retired unless you can use it in retirement. I'm not looking for a job.

No other interviewees supported this highly instrumental view of learning. In common with the participants, all the male non-participants enjoyed radio and television, particularly football and quiz programmes, although they also stressed that they were selective in choosing what they watched; and all except the blind interviewee read newspapers with considerable interest and undertook what one described as 'light reading'. Another also mentioned reading all he could about organic farming. The blind interviewee enjoyed travel talks on the radio and, as already discussed, benefited greatly from the availability of talking books. He also composed poetry.

Several of those who were still in reasonably good health appeared to be very active in a number of local clubs and societies where an element of learning was involved in the activities although the interviewees had generally not thought about this in these terms before. This included membership of a local fuchsia society, a camera club, competition bowling, a golf club, a jazz group and a family history group. Another man cited the Advanced Driving Group he had joined 'after one or two near scrapes' in order to update his driving skills. After some thought, one man also cited the travel he frequently undertook with his wife as a resource for learning. Indeed, it was notable that far more examples of informal learning than had been recorded in the questionnaires now began to emerge.

Interestingly, in both groups, two of the male interviewees stressed the importance of maintaining activity of some kind in retirement by comparing themselves to their fathers. One commented forcefully: 'When my old man retired – he retired on his 65th birthday and he was dead at 67 and I thought this isn't going to happen to me and I prepared for it.' It would be interesting to discover the extent to which this kind of experience encourages older people, especially older men, to ensure that they remain active post-work.

Of the six non-participant women, four had considered taking up a formal course of some kind but had not done so, either because they had recently moved to a new area or their interests were not provided for locally. One felt it would anyway 'be too much of a commitment' and was concerned that she might 'show her ignorance' although she had attended a woodwork class with her sister in the recent past. Another had already completed an Open University degree but felt that she did not possess a naturally enquiring mind and preferred to be 'force fed'. However, others were able to articulate possible interests they would like to explore including swimming and embroidery should the opportunity arise, although, like the men, most stressed that they 'already do a lot of other activities'. Examples given ranged from those conducted alone at home such as 'making things' and cookery to attending concerts and talks, exploring the countryside, discovering the history of the local village and walking. Observing wildlife was also popular, with one woman explaining that 'nature unfolds as you walk the dog'. Like the men, these women had not previously thought about these activities as 'learning' until prompted but began to reflect on this possibility during the interviews.

Interviewees were asked whether the informal learning in which they had now revealed themselves to be involved was the same as formal learning in a class or course. Responses were generally given unhesitatingly, with only one male and one female participant and one male non-participant unable to decide, with three non-responses overall. All the other participants except two women felt that the informal learning they had described was just as much valuable 'learning' as that undertaken in a formal situation in that 'it keeps the brain active' or they stressed that all kinds of learning 'keep you busy and alive' or felt that 'life is all learning.' Another woman stated simply: 'If it's something you don't know about and then you start to know about it, then that's learning.' This view was largely echoed by the non-participants, with one woman pointing out that 'you never stop acquiring new knowledge' whilst another felt it was 'an exchange of views' that was the key feature of both kinds of learning.

As noted previously, social activities were highly significant in some of the interviewees' lives. At this point, the participants described and discussed in more detail the range of social activities they enjoyed in addition to their courses and classes. For the women, these included 'meeting people in town' or talking with others through a communal supper at a worship group; staying in touch with old friends as well as 'catching up with other people's news'; membership of a retirement group or luncheon club related to their previous employment; 'getting to know other people' through membership of a rambling club; and attending talks through the local Women's Institute or regular voluntary work. The woman who was a carer for her son talked at length about carers' group outings including a 'pamper day' and how she had been helped through 'swapping information and realizing you still have a life of your own'. Two of the divorced participant women said they had no time available for any kind of regular group but did enjoy cinema and theatre visits, usually with a particular friend with whom they could discuss what they had seen. Certainly, getting together with friends for outings of various kinds and for stimulating discussion was especially pleasurable and important for all the women whatever their personal circumstances.

Three of the male participants also talked enthusiastically about social activities, including one who enjoyed 'hearing all the news' at meetings of a lottery syndicate that had grown out of his former firm's retired employees' club. Another was considering becoming a volunteer in a communal home and was aware that there were now far more activities available to older people. As described, some of the non-participants also belonged to social groups but both sexes were more inclined to favour occasional activities involving a speaker or 'expert' and those where there were opportunities for 'meeting people' and 'talking to people' as a way of 'getting more out of life'. The four women and three men who did not identify themselves as belonging to any kind of group nevertheless stressed that they enjoyed talking to and discussing issues with friends and acquaintances. Certainly, 'conversation and stimulation' were important for everyone, but not wishing to go out at night or health issues were given as reasons for not participating in more social activities in some cases.

Interviewees were asked to consider whether these social activities were the same as or different from learning activities. All of them considered this question very carefully, often giving detailed reasons for their replies. Overall, only four of the participants and two of the non-participants felt that they were the same although three other participants thought there was 'some overlap' and one woman observed that 'it depends on how you define learning', the first time this issue had actually been voiced.

Those who felt they were much the same tended to be those who had previously taken a holistic view of learning opportunities, commenting again that 'it's all learning' or that in both situations, 'you're meeting people and it's providing a learning experience' and 'it's keeping an active mind'. The majority who disagreed with this view, most of whom were currently participants, saw learning as more organized, purposeful, intense and requiring concentration even if it was taking place in an informal setting. Other interviewees who felt that social activities were more 'light-hearted and fun' explained that 'you're relaxed and don't have to have your mind in high gear'. However, two interviewees commented that formally organized learning opportunities also frequently offered the chance to socialize so that there was always some overlap.

The significance of learning

The participants were specifically asked how important learning was in their lives now, and some interesting views emerged. Three of the married women participants saw learning as 'quite' or 'very' important, as did all the other females, with one widow saying it was 'absolutely vital' and that she 'couldn't envisage life without it'. One of the divorced women felt that, although it was 'not required', it was personally important to her in that her classes provided 'a marker for the week'. The men were also very positive, stressing again that learning 'is round you all the time'. An enthusiastic female participant recalled a particularly salutary experience.

> I once read something in a sociology book that you never stop learning until the day you die because even if you are in a hospital bed dying you are still learning how to behave in that situation. You don't scream and yell because it would disturb other patients. You're constantly adding to your stock of learning.

However, the other married women and one man talked more in terms of the importance of 'keeping the brain ticking over' and the need to carry on learning 'until the brain gives out', suggesting that they had imbibed health messages about keeping mentally active. As one woman put it: 'You learn different things all the time. As you get older you do feel that you must do things that will keep the brain active. We've always got it at the back of our minds that we'll go ga-ga.' The non-participants, with the exception of the man who saw learning as job-related, nevertheless also felt that the learning they did in the course of their daily lives was important to them. After some thought, one widowed man who now revealed himself to be 88 years old, began to reflect on the woodwork centre he attended four mornings a week under the auspices of Age Concern and spoke about using his knowledge to help others:

> I not only enjoy being able to make things myself but I enjoy being able to help others to achieve the same sort of thing. They are very appreciative of anything I can do. My life revolves round that. An elderly lady brought in a sort of old sewing box . . . it was a family heirloom and it had fallen to pieces . . . and the person in charge there asked me if I would have a go at it. Fetching it all to pieces, restoring it and putting it back together again and then when the lady came in to see me, she was so overjoyed. She said it looked better than when it was new. The pleasure I got from seeing her face, it was really great.

Learning logs

As noted previously, the learning logs were designed to gain a better understanding of the types and amount of learning older people may do, particularly any informal learning activity, much of which goes unnoticed even by older people themselves as had emerged in the interviews. However, several of the learning logs were returned incomplete with entries ranging from four weeks' data to the full eight or nine weeks. In total, 63 weeks of data were recorded (mean = seven weeks of data) with 274 examples of learning activity being logged. We then divided the types of learning reported into formal learning activity and informal learning activity. Each category was subsequently broken down into a number of sub-categories including examples of 'creativity' and 'revision' as learning activities. Thus we were able to analyse the types of learning activities undertaken, in terms of both the source of learning and the topics themselves. This was a somewhat complex procedure but useful in helping to illuminate diarists' perceptions. We had also intended to calculate the number of hours each week spent in both formal and informal learning activity but only seven of the nine diarists tried to estimate this and it ultimately proved too difficult to assess with any degree of accuracy.

Types of learning

Analysis revealed 87 examples of formal learning activity (32 per cent). These included lectures 17 per cent (n = 15), classes 44 per cent (n = 38), organized groups 29 per cent (n = 25), and workshops or one-on-one sessions 10 per cent (n = 9). The majority of the examples were related to participation in art and design activity, including photography, 34 per cent (n = 30). If all the arts are taken together (art, literature and music) they accounted for 54 per cent of the formal learning activity undertaken (n = 47).

Computer classes accounted for 13 per cent (n = 11) of the formal learning, followed by lectures or one-to-one sessions related to health, 11 per cent (n = 10), particularly learning about health issues associated with growing older. Learning as part of a history group (n = 7) or Bible study group (n = 6) were also popular activities within the formal learning environment. Other topics approached in formal learning environments included natural history (n = 3), with current affairs, science and craft each logged once. One diarist observed that 'the courses structure my week and provide stimulus for further activity/research'.

As with the interviewees, diarists who did not attend classes or courses offered explanations with a typical reason being 'at this stage in my life I do not choose to actively go to many classes to take in information'. The inference here is that learning informally offers learners the opportunity to play a more active part in the learning process. Certainly, of the 274 entries, 59 per cent (n = 161) were considered to represent examples of informal learning. Sources of this informal learning were categorized into eight sub-categories (Box 5.1). Interpersonal relationships were also logged as a

---

Box 5.1   Sources of informal learning

- Television
- Radio
- Publications
- Internet
- Theatre and/or cinema
- Museums and/or heritage centres
- Peers or colleagues
- Other family members

source of informal learning (11 per cent, n = 18). These accounts were divided into learning through interaction with peers (n = 14) or colleagues and learning through family members (n = 4).

The majority of informal learning, 35 per cent (n = 56), was concerned with aspects of history and/or natural history. Most of this was achieved through watching television documentaries and wildlife programmes. Indeed, the degree of informal learning undertaken related to natural history may have been significantly higher than the learning logs show, given the admission by one interviewee that he had an ongoing interest in wildlife programmes but had not thought to mention just how many he watched.

The arts made up 21 per cent (n = 34) of the informal learning recorded, with current affairs and 'general knowledge' accounting for 17 per cent (n = 28). Much of this appeared to be acquired through diarists' enjoyment of regular television quiz programmes that allowed them to pit their wits against contestants. Learning informally about health, especially relating to the process of ageing, accounted for 6 per cent of the examples logged, as did scientific topics. Learning about religious topics and crafts each accounted for 1 per cent of the informal learning logged. Other topics covered by informal learning activity included gardening (5 per cent) and cooking (2 per cent). Interestingly, there were no examples logged of computing as informal learning. This is probably due to the classification of revision and practice activities as different from other types of informal learning as they tended to accompany learning activities already undertaken in formally organized computer classes.

Fewer than 7 per cent (n = 11) of the informal learning examples were related to topics such as reminiscence, life review and changing roles in later life. This kind of learning usually took place incidentally during conversation and/or activities with peers or family members. It is possible that it was not always seen as learning and therefore not necessarily logged by every diarist.

There were 26 entries (9 per cent) that did not fit neatly into the formal/ informal classifications. These included revision for word processing exams, practising musical pieces, creating original works of poetry and some craft activities. It was unclear from the logs whether these examples were always related to some aspect of formal learning or represented stand-alone learning undertaken by the individual.

The findings from the learning logs highlight the extent to which learning in later life is much more than engagement in formal learning activities since less than one-third of the learning reported in the logs took place in formal learning environments. The findings also emphasize the diverse ways in which older people continue to engage in learning activities and the variety of topics they consider as part of that learning. Taken together, evidence from the interviews and the logs also demonstrate that, whilst some topics such as computing are better studied formally with opportunities for additional practice learning on an individual basis, others such as natural history lend themselves to learning mainly through television. Again, subjects such as art and literature can be approached both formally and informally. This finding may be related to the nature of the topic, to older people's particular circumstances or it may be a reflection of individual learning style preferences developed over many years.

Finally, the process of keeping the log raised awareness in many of the diarists as to the role and significance of learning in their lives, as the following quotes illustrate.

> As a result of keeping this log I realise how my learning is virtually non-stop . . . books, TV, radio and human interaction, as well as formal learning sessions.

> No need to 'wind-down' so far as learning is concerned!

Conclusion

In this chapter, we have listened to what older people have to say about their post-work lives and the role of learning, and have also analysed what kinds of learning a small group of them actually undertake over a set period. Our conclusion is that, if our findings are representative of older people in general, the kinds of learning in which they are involved post-work are wide-ranging and very varied, and certainly appear to have no limits! In the next chapter, we will move forward in time to examine the current social and policy context for later life learning and will then consider the main themes that have emerged from our study, updating our model to take account of what we have learnt.

Chapter 6

New contexts, new learners?

Introduction

The concept of time in its different forms provided a useful framework for our examination of the kind of life course factors that have impacted on many older people's experiences of learning and their choices about learning in later life. Because some years have elapsed since our study was carried out, it is instructive at this point to consider further how the policy context for later life learning has changed in the intervening years specifically within the UK and to consider the factors that have come to affect the education of adults in general, and the opportunities open to older learners in particular. Against this background, we will examine some themes that derive from our fieldwork and present a new version of our model of life course learning.

In the opening chapter, we examined some international policy developments in lifelong learning and considered some of the academic debates and perspectives that have emerged around the concept. We also briefly considered the global demographic shift towards population ageing and some of the policy responses, noting that any rationale for enabling older people to access learning opportunities has come to emphasize both engagement and inclusion, sometimes underpinned by a sense of individual responsibility. We further noted some of the difficulties inherent in the promotion of lifestyle choice and opportunity in respect of later life learning. In considering policy developments within the UK since our study was originally completed, it is difficult to escape the conclusion that these difficulties have multiplied within the intervening years and that the current picture is fraught with contradictions and tensions. However, as we shall see, the beginnings of some more positive developments can be perceived.

Changes in the policy context for later life learning

In our opening chapter, we pointed out that our study was originally conceived at a time when, although lifelong learning appeared to offer some kind of panacea for the perceived deficits in the educational system in the UK in view of the rapidly changing social and economic climate, older people actually received very little attention and were more or less excluded from consideration regarding educational opportunities. Since then, as we have seen, they have become the focus of a whole range of international and national policy statements and developments as the potential impact of demographic trends becomes a reality. The importance of learning for personal, civic and social purposes and the promotion of active ageing to include opportunities to learn and now strongly promoted through the European Commission's latest programmes, has also come to be widely stressed in a range of recent UK policy documents that address issues pertaining to the ageing population.

Among these has been the government's somewhat belated acknowledgement of the challenges posed by the growth of people over 50 in the UK population and their proposed strategy for promoting active ageing. In 2008, it was announced that Dame Joan Bakewell, a former television personality and now a journalist and writer, was to take on the role of the Voice of Older People at the age of 76 to represent older people's views to central government on matters of concern. Some questions have been raised as to the usefulness of this post but it does at least represent an acknowledgement of older people's sheer weight of numbers and potential influence in the political arena.

Official recognition of the benefits learning can bring was set out in the document *Opportunity Age* (HM Government 2005). Here the government addressed a range of issues concerning different aspects of older people's lives and put forward its intentions for measures designed to improve their quality of life. Notably, it appeared to commit itself to ensuring the availability of a wide range of learning and leisure opportunities for older people in spite of an open acknowledgement that some adult learners, including older people, might have to pay more for their courses in the longer term. It was also recognized that there is a variation in the availability of opportunities and in fees charged in different parts of the UK but it was considered appropriate that this should prevail in view of varying local needs and circumstances. However, it was not clarified how these local needs could be assessed and understood.

A second volume of this publication that tried to produce a social portrait of ageing in the UK also observed that 'around 35 per cent of people in their sixties undertake taught learning' (HM Government 2008: 25), although it was not stated what forms of learning this includes. However, a more recent report from the Audit Commission notes that although the *Opportunity Age* initiative was designed to improve older people's quality of life it has had 'limited impact' (Audit Commission 2008: 6). The Commission further observed that England's local authorities are not doing enough to ensure that the ageing population has sufficient interesting and worthwhile activities with which to engage in spite of some excellent examples of good practice. A particular criticism was that councils are not making it easy for older people to access information about learning opportunities or leisure and social activities and volunteering.

Although a revised version of *Opportunity Age* is promised for the future, it is not yet known what position it will take. There has, however, been a partial attempt to address the issues raised. Following on from *Opportunity Age*, the now defunct Social Exclusion Unit argued for the need for a comprehensive approach for developing accessible joined-up services for older people in order to address social exclusion issues. Lifelong learning was identified as one important strand of this in *A Sure Start to Later Life: Ending Inequalities for Older People* (Office of the Deputy Prime Minister 2006). The *LinkAge Plus* pilot programme that followed was designed to test this joined-up approach through eight partnership pilots in both urban and rural areas with older people themselves involved in design and delivery. NIACE itself produced a comprehensive briefing sheet to assist the pilots in considering how and when later life learning could be offered, consisting of a series of actions that the pilots might consider, going beyond simply pointing older people in the direction of existing educational provision. Yet, although the external evaluation of the pilots was generally favourable (Ritters and Davis 2008), the opportunity to promote learning appears to have been lost.

The Department of Health has also used the theme of active ageing as a way of promoting the health and well-being of the ageing population. The vital role of learning in later life was acknowledged in a series of policy documents, notably in Standard 8 of *The National Service Framework (NSF) for Older People* (Department of Health 2001) where the availability of education and leisure activities was seen as an important factor in helping to prevent illness in later life. Other Department of Health programmes, such as *Better Health in Old Age* (2004) and the *Partnerships for Older People* (POPPS) projects launched in 2006, demonstrated how learning, especially in relation to health issues, is a vital component of the Department's policy for older people that emphasizes social inclusion, control by older people themselves and encouragement to be active, healthy and independent for longer, hopefully resulting in an enhanced quality of life.

What is noticeable here is that, in England at least, until comparatively recently policy statements have mainly emanated from government departments 'other than education which remained surprisingly quiet on the issue of later life learning' (Withnall 2008: 14) although the Department of Education previously funded some aspects of NIACE's work with older people and also co-operated with some of the Department of Health's initiatives. Certainly, the reality is that even greater numbers of older learners, and indeed, adult learners in general, appear to have been lost to publicly funded education at a range of levels on account of various changes in government educational policies over the last few years. Indeed, Coffield, in a general article commenting critically on government policy in respect of post-compulsory education overall, remarks particularly on the 'avalanches of policy pouring down on the [adult education] system' noting that 'over the last twenty years there have been fifteen junior Ministers and fifteen different civil servants in charge' (2008: 10).

In 2007, NIACE estimated that a million adults had disappeared from publicly funded adult learning since 2005 with the greatest loss being in the numbers of people over the age of 65, although the Department of Innovation, Universities and Skills (DIUS) itself does not keep precise figures. Whilst numbers of these learners were now less than half the totals in further education in 2004–5, they were also 30 per cent lower in activities funded through what the government calls its personal and community development learning budget (Aldridge and Tuckett 2007).

The drop in numbers has been compounded through the implementation of the recommendations of the *Leitch Review of Skills*, the final report of which was published in 2006 (HM Treasury 2006). The report recommended that the UK should commit to becoming a world leader in skills by 2020 with a series of targets for adults of working age and a radical change in funding and operation across the whole skills spectrum and with different implications for infrastructure, policy and targets in each of the devolved administrations of the UK. Whilst the proposed changes are designed to lead to a more prosperous and productive society overall, critics have argued that, as more of the adult learning budget is diverted into prescribed skills training, we have inevitably moved away from New Labour's original commitment to the principles of lifelong learning even if these were never fully implemented.

It is not entirely clear how far the loss of some older learners from publicly funded education can also be attributed to the implementation of the Employment Equality (Age) Act 2006 that pertains to England, Wales and Scotland with associated legislation in Northern Ireland. Part of the legislation forbids discrimination in the provision of education and training on grounds of age. Since age-related fee concessions clearly discriminate against younger people, they must be objectively justified or covered by an exemption. Accordingly, educators devising courses aimed specifically at older people would have to show that their aim is to remedy some age-related disadvantage that members of that age group suffer. Providers may therefore be able to make a case for providing concessions for older people for whom these kinds of educational opportunities were unavailable earlier in their lives but, in some parts of the UK, the legislation initially resulted in some confusion as to how it should be interpreted in respect of concessionary fees for older people. Several English local authorities used the legislation to abolish concessionary fees completely, with the result that their courses and classes were often financially beyond the reach of older students.

A further move was the decision implemented in 2008 to cut £100 million of funding for students wishing to study for a higher education qualification at the same or a lower level if they already possess such a qualification (ELQ). Again, the money saved was to be reallocated to those studying for a first higher education qualification in order to help widen participation and to boost the skills of the workforce. Opponents of the scheme argued that this policy affects large numbers of part-time students and may accordingly hit potential older learners (although these are defined as those aged 35 and over!) including those who may have acquired a qualification in the past but who now wish to retrain for a new career or for voluntary work or, indeed, to study a new subject at an advanced level for pleasure. There were certainly those among our study participants who had previously obtained a qualification and who might now be financially prevented from studying at a similar or lower level in future should they so wish. On the other hand, this policy, coupled with the removal in 2006 of the upper age limit for eligibility for loans for higher education fees, may enable other older people, if previously unqualified, to undertake study up to degree level assuming they can pay costs or afford repayments. Admittedly, it is unlikely that this would have benefited many of the people in our study but it may be helpful for other older people in future especially if they are remaining in the labour market and are seeking progression in their careers or looking for a change of direction.

Of course, some older people may now have chosen to undertake other forms of learning not always amenable to quantification; it is notable that the University of the Third Age has reported a considerable growth in membership in recent years. However, the extent to which older people's personal learning interests (and the 'leisure learning' of adult learners in general) have been largely overlooked in the quest to address the UK's perceived skills deficit with its accompanying diversion of the adult learning budget is only too apparent.

Indeed, concern over the kind of support needed for adult learning in general in today's changing society and the role of the state in enabling it is currently the focus of a Commission of Inquiry into the Future for Lifelong Learning established by NIACE and with a number of leading experts in government, business, public service and academia acting as commissioners. Although independent of NIACE, the Commission's terms of reference are wide and include recognition of the need to 'effect a cultural shift in the value attached by policy-makers and the public to adult learning' (NIACE 2007: 9). The Commission also acknowledges the potential of adult learning 'towards securing a future characterized by economic prosperity; social justice, social cohesion and personal well-being; and environmental sustainability in the UK' (NIACE 2007: 9). This appears to represent the multi-faceted approach to lifelong learning advocated by Aspin and Chapman (2007) and discussed in Chapter 1.

Noting the problem of giving a meaning to lifelong learning, the Commission chose to adopt a thematic approach to its inquiry. Of the ten themes selected, one relates to demographic change and the learning needs that an ageing society generates as well as exploring migration, changing career and family patterns and the needs of those who will become adults in future. The Commission provided a preliminary paper on this theme (McNair 2007) and held an early expert seminar to discuss the issues raised (see www.lifelonglearninginquiry.org.uk).

After the Commission was announced, a major development was the launch, early in 2008, of a government consultation on what it called 'informal learning' perhaps as a result of widely expressed concern over the demise of publicly funded adult education but also in recognition that methods of learning for adults in general have become considerably more diverse than in the past, especially with the growth of information technology. The consultation used a different definition of informal learning from ours; here it is seen as 'structured or non-structured part-time, non-vocational learning, which does not lead to qualifications – or at least where qualifications are incidental to the learning' (DIUS 2008: 5). The consultation's aim was to encourage exploration and debate of a whole range of questions grouped under five subheadings (see Box 6.1).

Box 6.1   Informal adult learning: shaping the way ahead

- Understanding and improving on current provision
- The government contribution
- DIUS-funded informal adult education
- Equality of access
- Broadcasting and technology

(DIUS 2008)

The consultation received more than five thousand responses in a comparatively short time. When these were analysed, there seemed to be some surprise that 'older learners are among the most numerous contributors to the consultation' (COI 2008: 17). To what extent was this response from so many older people illustrative of their dismay at the increased cost of, or indeed loss of, local learning opportunities? There were certainly some specific comments about the beneficial effects of non-vocational learning in later life that were very much in accord with our own findings especially with regards to increasing knowledge and skills and social interaction. Some providers also commented on the removal of fee concessions as a result of a particular interpretation of the Employment Equality (Age) Regulations 2006 as previously discussed. Other older respondents advocated local strategies to tackle this and other problems that made it difficult to access local learning opportunities and argued for older people to have a role in contributing to the development of such local strategies.

Overall, DIUS's initial response to the consultation acknowledged the need for strong local partnerships, to ensure 'connectivity' between different types of learning and to reach out to potential learners, especially those who have had least access in the past and are now least able to fund their own learning. There was also recognition of the importance of self-organized learning and the potential of technology to support learning but only as 'one of a range of delivery mechanisms' (COI 2008: 27). Nevertheless, there was recognition of the fact that many older people are reluctant to engage with information technology and do not see the need for it at this stage of their lives. This was the case for some of those in our study, although others were keen to develop computer skills. Finally, the consultation produced a number of broad suggestions for building on what is already in place and, whilst not denying the role of professional teachers, the significant contribution that volunteers can make, illustrated in the U3A model, was also acknowledged.

The government intends to respond formally with a new policy document in due course so that it is likely that there will be some new developments in the ways that learning for all adults is recognized, funded and organized in coming years. Meanwhile, a range of around fifty other bodies, not all of them educational in focus, joined together to form the Campaigning Alliance for Lifelong Learning (CALL), officially launched late in 2008 (see www.callcampaign.org.uk). Briefly, CALL members believe that the education system should provide a range of opportunities for all adult learners, including learning for personal well-being and development. They advocate the maintenance of local authority adult education and learner, teacher and community involvement in all levels of decision-making. These demands seem particularly pertinent to older learners in view of the kinds of formal learning in which some of our study participants were involved. There are plans to involve CALL's members in further developing the government's responses to the consultation in view of the passionate commitment to adult learning they have shown, but it is not yet clear how this will happen or what the overall outcomes will be.

Later life learning in the devolved administrations

Lifelong learning in its role as a vital component of the mission to make the UK competitive in the global economy has also largely informed educational policies in the UK's devolved administrations, Northern Ireland, Wales and Scotland. However, in respect of opportunities to learn in later life, they have also had the opportunity to consider the nature of appropriate provision in respect of their own particular populations' needs. Although Northern Ireland has largely followed the UK government's lead in its concentration on the development of vocational education, it has a long-term strategy in place to support the inclusion of older people as part of its overall anti-poverty strategy, itself designed to develop an integrated approach for tackling financial, economic and social exclusion. As yet, however, there has been no direct mention of the possibilities of lifelong learning in respect of older people. It is a voluntary organization, the Workers Educational Association Northern Ireland (WEA-NI), that has taken the lead in expanding provision for socially excluded older people in different parts of the province through its *Learning Age Project* with financial support from an external body (www.wea-ni.com).

There are, however, more promising developments in both Wales and Scotland. Grounded in the UN Principles for Older People, the *Strategy for Older People in Wales* (Welsh Assembly Government 2003) has as one of its aims the promotion and development of older people's capacity to go on working and learning and to contribute actively to their communities following retirement. An extensive programme for education and lifelong learning is in place, with the aims of removing barriers to learning and encouraging people over 50 back into learning as well as boosting the development of information technology skills in local communities. The strategy was backed by a ten-year framework for action and supported by dedicated funding over a five-year period. A Commissioner for Older People was appointed in 2008 to oversee older people's varied interests and a version of the strategy to cover the period 2008–13 has now been produced (Welsh Assembly Government 2008a).

Scotland already had a lifelong learning strategy in place when the Scottish Executive (now known as the Scottish Government) produced details of its strategic approach to planning for a Scotland with an ageing population, *All Our Futures. Planning for a Scotland with an Ageing Population* (Scottish Executive 2007). The comprehensive vision set out for older people's lives is largely based on the principle that age should not be used to make assumptions about people's value and individual contribution to society. The action plan described includes both actions to be taken by the government and invitations to other bodies to participate, together with criteria for evaluation for success. In respect of later life learning, the particularly important elements relate to older people having access to information technology and the internet and being able to take part in learning activities, whether these are for vocational purposes or for personal development.

It is particularly interesting that both Wales and Scotland have acknowledged the importance of intergenerational activity, echoing Article 14 of the Madrid declaration (2002) that addresses the importance of intergenerational links. The Welsh Assembly Government has published a consultation document, *Building a Society for All Ages. Draft Intergenerational Practice Strategy for Wales* (Welsh Assembly Government 2008b), although there already exists a Welsh Centre for Intergenerational Practice set up at the University of Glamorgan, a large network of organizations interested in intergenerational practice and an accredited intergenerational course at the University of Wales Lampeter. The University of Strathclyde in Glasgow, active for two decades in providing learning activities for people over 50, is also hosting a new Scottish Centre for Intergenerational Practice in conjunction with Children in Scotland. As in Wales, the Centre intends to work with a range of individuals and organizations to help develop intergenerational work across Scotland.

Both the Welsh and Scottish Centres for Intergenerational Practice were set up with the assistance of the original Centre for Intergenerational Practice (CIP) founded in 2001 by the Beth Johnson Foundation based in Stoke-on-Trent in the UK, although a pioneering organization, Generations Together, has been in existence at the University of Pittsburgh in the USA for some years. CIP's aim is to support the further development of intergenerational practice and to promote the potential of intergenerational approaches as a way of addressing social issues. Indeed, there is now an International Consortium for Intergenerational Programmes that brings together people who are interested in advancing intergenerational practice worldwide (www.incip.info/), and an international journal exists to enable the sharing of good practice and to encourage debate. Intergenerational activity may well be one very positive way of ensuring that older people remain visible within their societies and are enabled to go on contributing to both their own well-being and that of other generations.

Other developments in later life learning

Beyond those that are publicly funded, a variety of other learning opportunities for older people have appeared since our study was completed, although it would be a separate task to survey the whole field. However, since some of our study participants were enthusiastic members of U3A, it is worth noting the considerable expansion in people learning via this self-help route, so that, towards the end of 2008, there were over seven hundred groups with almost 21,000 members in the UK according to the Third Age Trust (www.u3a.org.uk/). There are also some other U3A groups that operate independently of the Trust as well as a whole range of activities across the UK, often run by voluntary organizations or charities and incorporating opportunities to learn alongside a range of 'leisure' activities. Certainly, many of our interviewees appreciated the availability of these kinds of facilities within their local areas; and NIACE's *Older and Bolder* project has revealed the extent to which innovative and imaginative provision for older learners has flourished in some places. Some of our interviewees were also engaged in learning through their place of worship, although the extent to which this happens across the UK remains largely undocumented.

Many of our study participants pursued learning through creative activities, and there appears to have been an expansion of provision for this over the last few years, whether on a small scale at local level or through activities such as those offered for older people through various

Arts Council England active ageing projects around the country (www. artscouncil.org). Overall, work by Aldridge and Tuckett (2007) on older people's learning, based on data from the NIACE survey of adult partici- pation in learning in 2005, confirms that older people (defined here in ten-year age bands from age 45 to 75 plus) are involved in an enormous range of learning activities whether still in paid work or not. Opportunities to acquire computer skills were particularly important for their respon- dents, as we found among some of the older people in our own study. However, we also saw that this is not necessarily true for all older people. As Withnall *et al.* (2004) have observed elsewhere, it is likely that there are still very large numbers of older people who do not have access to a computer or who are held back by fear of failure in confronting unfamiliar and what can appear to be very complex procedures.

Older learners in a changing context

Returning to our model, we have seen that time has brought a range of changes to the framework for lifelong learning and to later life learning in particular. The original government commitment to lifelong learning as a cradle-to-grave entitlement, even if never fully operationalized, now appears to have been largely abandoned although the government is keen to show its commitment to what it currently terms 'informal adult learning'. Although there has been wide recognition of the value of later life learning from a range of different agencies and from the devolved governments in Wales and Scotland, the nature of the educational opportunities available has changed over recent years with the result that we are at something of a crossroads in considering what direction should be taken in respect of later life learning. Accordingly, it is helpful to use our model to focus further on later life itself and to consider three interrelated themes that have emerged from our study in respect of later life learning. Nevertheless, it has to be acknowledged that the external framework is likely to change again over time; and that successive cohorts of older people will continue to be diverse in their backgrounds, experiences, expectations and aspira- tions. Hence our acknowledgement of new contexts and new learners in the title of this chapter.

Theme 1: the importance of life course influences

It was apparent from the findings of our focus groups and confirmed in the later parts of our study that a range of contextual, collective, situational and individual influences interact in an extremely complex and generally unpredictable manner to influence people's propensity to learn across the life course. It is therefore extremely difficult to assess the relative importance of each influence on the individual although, within our 'time' framework, family background, gender, experiences of education and learning (especially early in life) and the timing of becoming post-work appear to have been important factors, as well as situational influences in retirement such as location and living arrangements. We were unable to explore the impact of race and ethnicity in any detail beyond the focus groups and this needs further consideration. However, the evidence we obtained through our study partly illuminates the later findings of Gorard and Selwyn (2005), who analysed data from 1001 structured interviews with adults in the UK, 352 of whom were aged 60 or over. They argued that patterns of participation in education and training across the life course can be predicted to some extent, with the key social determinants of lifelong participation in learning being time, place, sex, family and initial schooling, with family background being particularly influential. However, from our study, there are some additional points to be made.

Many of our study participants stressed their lifetime commitment to learning, and some of the focus group members in particular believed that their own personality traits helped them to remain focused and resilient in dealing with the various aspects of disruption and change that they had encountered during their lives. Even if they did not currently identify themselves as learners, other study participants were generally well able to reflect back across their lives and to identify what they believed to be changing social and cultural norms in society across time and the influences and experiences that had accordingly shaped their beliefs, expectations and the opportunities available to them at different times. They were also able to discuss some future possibilities they had considered for themselves or, in a few cases, to talk perceptively about how things might change for them over time.

From the perspective of developmental psychology, Russell (2008) describes this self-awareness as the desire to maintain integrity and continuity of the self over time. As she found in her study of older computer students in Australia, learning in later life was a way of remaining active but, more importantly for these learners, it helped to maintain the intellectual curiosity and stimulation they had recognized in themselves since childhood. Like Russell's interviewees, some of our learners acknowledged this trait in themselves and sought out ways to continue their learning even when they were currently unable or unwilling to participate in a class, whilst others could not easily envisage a life in which learning in some form did not feature prominently. For example, we saw that one interviewee was still able to go on learning through the services of his local library even after losing his sight. It may be that personality factors have been largely overlooked in understanding what influences older people to persevere with learning even when their situational and individual circumstances appear to be adverse.

In addition, as we noted earlier, Dench and Regan (2000) found in their own study of motivation to learn in later life that appearing to be a non-learner or non-participant is not necessarily a static status. Certainly, some of those older people whom we had designated as 'non-participants' had studied formally in the past or had thought about doing so in future. We previously described them as 'serial learners'. Additionally, many people were involved in a whole range of learning-related activities at any one time, both formal and informal, and often through hobbies or interests sparked off by chance; this had been a pattern for many of them in the past and most expected it to continue. Such people might be termed 'life-wide learners' who see learning as a holistic endeavour. Accordingly, we would now argue that it is important not to label older people as in some way inactive and non-participant without an understanding of their particular experiences, current circumstances and beliefs together with the availability of suitable opportunities at any one point in their lives and their ability and willingness to engage with them.

Theme 2: changing perspectives on learning

At the beginning of our study we deliberately refrained from defining what we meant by 'learning'. We have seen that those of our respondents whom we invited to offer a definition generally agreed that it was basically concerned with acquiring new knowledge and/or developing skills. However, connected to the conviction that learning is a lifelong process, a strong belief also emerged that in later life it is different from the kinds of learning experienced at earlier stages that was often undertaken out of necessity or because it was compulsory. Now learning becomes more personal and reflective and is more closely associated with what are experienced as its positive outcomes such as the maintenance of health and well-being as people age.

Related to this, it was apparent that learning was seen as having an important role in generally supporting people in dealing with aspects of growing older, especially keeping an active brain, whilst enabling them to remain connected to society. Ideas about maintaining an active and enquiring mind through learning and broadening horizons as well as sheer enjoyment and a sense of accomplishment were revealed as important factors, sometimes intertwined with the chance to meet people and make new friends. It may be that underlying these views concerning the necessity of maintaining mental activity, self-esteem and social contact is the fear of loss of cognitive function, openly expressed by one interviewee but possibly a much greater worry among older people than is commonly acknowledged. In stressing the importance of keeping an active mind, these study participants appeared to have internalized the popular message that 'exercising' the brain helps to guard against neurological illness in later life. The range of widely promoted 'brain training' opportunities currently available through both books and electronic games for adults of all ages may have fuelled this belief.

At present, there is some scepticism among some psychologists and neuroscientists as to the true value of this kind of mental exercise in warding off neurodegeneration. However, Salthouse (2006) has observed that the kind of activities in which many of our study participants were involved may be contributing to a higher quality of life through the sense of enjoyment they offer while simultaneously providing reassurance to the participant that they are still able to function satisfactorily. However, it is also important to help older people to understand that physical exercise and a healthy diet are major factors in maintaining good mental health as they age. In any case, they may need more reassurance that physiological deterioration of the brain and loss of functional capacity are not inevitable parts of ageing (Whitbourne 2001) as far as we know. The UK Medical Research Council (MRC) *Cognitive Function and Ageing Study*, a population-based, multi-centre study in England and Wales that is currently entering a new phase, will hopefully be able to shed more light on the possible connections between lifelong learning and the maintenance of good health in later life (www.cfas/ac/uk). We return to this issue in the next chapter.

In some cases, where learning was being undertaken formally it was sometimes acknowledged as being more purposeful than informal learning, valuable though this was. Some older people also preferred the kind of structured learning a course or class offers for exploring particular subjects that appear to lend themselves better to this mode of study. Even so, some of our respondents had come to realize that they now needed different ways for their formal learning to be organized, and conventional courses with emphasis on progression were not what they wanted. Others were more affected by factors in the learning environment and occasionally disappointed by a lack of facilities.

However, learning in later life does not necessarily depend on the avail-ability of a formal structure, witnessed by the amount of informal learning with which many people in our study were engaged. We have seen that many older people are able to use their life course experiences to explore a range of other ways to learn, including organizing their own learning by building on knowledge gained through work, through hobbies and interests that might be developed with a spouse or friend, or simply through having a new interest triggered spontaneously. Whatever its form, many of our study participants had come to believe that learning was an integral and important feature of their daily lives but recognized that it was qualitatively different from learning they had undertaken in the past.

Theme 3: variety in learning

We have touched above on the huge variety of topics and interests that engaged our study participants, whether they had chosen to follow a course or were learning informally or both. It appears that many older people maintain or develop a diversity of interests well into old age and enjoy learning in a range of different ways. In particular, detailed evidence from the learning logs illustrated in depth the sheer variety of learning older people undertake informally, even though some of them did not initially recognize this as learning until our questions encouraged them to reflect on their activities. Older people's involvement with a very wide range of learning activities and subjects has since been confirmed through analysis of a large dataset by Aldridge and Tuckett (2007).

We saw that many of our study participants, especially those in the focus groups, talked about having the time and freedom to plan and to make choices about their lives post-work even if the reality had turned out differently for some people. As Russell (2008) points out, however, there is a sense in which older people actually have less time because they are nearer to the end of their lives. Some of the older interviewees and some of those who kept learning logs tended to restrict their activities outside the home, preferring to learn through enjoyment of more home-based activities such as gardening, reading or watching television. However, on their own terms, they appeared to be leading fulfilling and creative lives in which learning featured prominently with no sense of finitude. Many of them demonstrated resilience and fortitude in the face of transitions that later life often brings. Although not everyone acknowledged that their activities might be construed as learning, they generally felt they were still developing as individuals and were anxious to stay in touch with the world. Indeed, those study participants who were formally learning to use a computer or study a new language demonstrated that many older people are keen to keep abreast of new developments and do not wish to be left behind. Unlike some of Russell's students and contrary to Laslett's vision for older people (1989), the majority of those taking part in our study did not seem particularly concerned with leaving a legacy for future generations; they were still too busy developing themselves even though they greatly valued contact with their families and derived considerable enjoyment from family activities.

A new model

Our study has demonstrated that the complex interplay of forces that were found to have influenced people's participation in education and learning over the life course continues to operate in later life although different factors come to the fore. As a result of our findings about the nature of the post-work situation and our analysis of the changes in educational and social policy that have emerged over time, we now present an updated model that incorporates changes in the balance of influences on learning in later life, together with an illustration of the outcomes our study has shown older people believe themselves to experience as a result of their learning activity. There may also be longer-term outcomes that they have not yet recognized. We believe the model has the potential to raise awareness of the need to take more account of the historical and social context of older people's lives and how this affects their engagement with learning

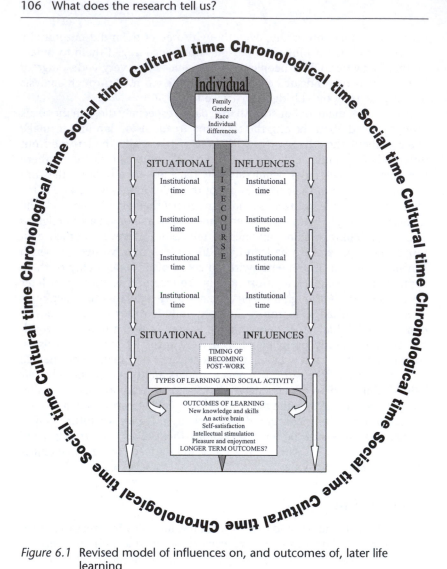

Figure 6.1 Revised model of influences on, and outcomes of, later life
learning

in all its forms as new cohorts of adults move into later life with their own
experiences and beliefs.

Conclusion

In this chapter we have traced the major developments in educational and
social policy in respect of lifelong learning across the UK since our study
was originally completed. We have noted how, in spite of some recognition

of the supposed value of learning in later life and some good intentions, older people still barely feature in educational thinking, and indeed non-vocational adult education has largely taken a back seat in the current drive to improve the skills of the workforce. Although we may expect some new developments in future, it is not yet clear what form these will take. We have also summarized the main themes that have emerged from our study and revised our model of some of the life course influences on older people's propensity to continue learning to incorporate findings from the later part of our study. In the final chapter, we will consider the overall implications of our study and identify some direction for further research.

Part III

What are the overall implications?

Chapter 7

A better future for older learners?

Introduction

Are there any further grounds for optimism in relation to learning in later life? We begin this final chapter by reconsidering the implications of our study in the light of a challenging new perspective on the role and potential of lifelong learning. We will then assess the contribution that our study has made to thinking specifically about later life learning, including the usefulness of adopting a life course approach. We will go on to make some suggestions as to how opportunities to learn in later life might be broadened and improved. Finally, we will identify some aspects that would benefit from further research in order to address some of the existing gaps in our knowledge.

Where is lifelong learning going?

We have seen that the contested concept of lifelong learning has undergone a number of transitions over its lifetime, especially in relation to its role in educational policy. In our study, however, it was apparent that the older people who took part were almost all wedded to an understanding of learning as something that takes place literally throughout life even though its meaning, function and form are subject to change at different points during the life course. They were also insightful in analysing the various benefits that they believed accrued from continuing to learn in later life, with particular emphasis on the maintenance of cognitive function and, in conjunction with other positive aspects of their lives, its role in helping to generate a general sense of contentment and well-being as they grew older.

It is worth noting that, since we began writing this book, this kind of thinking has emerged in the report of a major project from the Foresight Programme, part of the UK Government Office for Science (GO-Science) within DIUS. The Foresight Programme makes use of available evidence from a whole range of disciplines in the natural and social sciences to support strategic thinking and to help inform government policy across a variety of departments (www.foresight.gov.uk). The peer-reviewed *Foresight Mental*

Capacity and Wellbeing Project (2008) is concerned specifically with advising the government as to how the best possible development and optimum well-being might be achieved in future for everyone in the UK. As such, it provides a useful structure for considering policy development rather than offering a prescriptive account.

As in our model, we see here different aspects of change over time providing a framework for analysis. Underlying the project is a futuristic vision of the factors that will drive change over the next two decades, one of which is the demographic age profile. Other challenges to be faced are the changes in the global economy and in work; the changing make-up of UK society and evolving attitudes and expectations; the changing nature of public services; and the relentless growth of new science and technology that are continually changing the various ways in which we communicate and learn at different stages of life. However, the report's authors warn of the pressing need to ensure equality of access to new technologies rather than allowing them to bring about further divisions in society (Government Office for Science 2008). Although we would endorse this view, it is important to point out that, for older learners, access on its own would not be sufficient unless there was the kind of satisfactory instructional support that some of our study participants were receiving at the time in a formally organized class but with other opportunities for practice. As Withnall *et al.* (2004) have previously observed, some older people may also need train-ing materials that are user-friendly in that they take account of possible age-related impairments and allow learners to work at their own pace. Then there are particular requirements for those whose first language is not English, although there have been some initial moves to address this issue through Age Concern.

The report makes use of two aspects of mental development that make up 'mental capital' to formulate its approach. The first of these relates to mental capacity that 'encompasses a person's cognitive and emotional resources' and includes their level of efficiency at learning as well as their social skills and degree of resilience when dealing with stress. The second is mental well-being which is concerned with the individual being enabled 'to develop their potential' and to 'work productively and creatively' as well as forging good relationships with others and contributing to their community (Government Office for Science 2008: 10). For our purposes, it is particularly apposite that one of the key findings of the project is the importance of learning throughout life in that it is said to directly affect mental health and well-being across all age groups. Accordingly, 'boosting brainpower' at all ages through different kinds of interventions is recom-mended. The underlying rationale is that how a nation develops and makes use of its mental capital can have a far-reaching effect on its economic competitiveness and overall prosperity as well as having significant impli-cations for social inclusion and cohesion (Beddington *et al.* 2008).

This integrated lifetime perspective that acknowledges the importance of interventions in childhood, in adult working life and in respect of the ageing population certainly offers a more inclusive route to the achievement of some of the kind of policy aims that we examined in the opening chapter. However, it can be criticized on the grounds that a concentration on mental capital is doing little more than adding another narrowly focused dimension to interpretations of lifelong learning that ultimately focus on economic outcomes with only secondary consideration of other rationales. In any case, the assumed causal link between the development of mental capital and social inclusion and cohesion appears to be somewhat simplistic and needs further exploration and debate.

The project report nevertheless makes a particularly strong case for 'unlocking the mental capacity in older people and promoting their well-being' (Government Office for Science 2008: 34). It is argued that learning through the life course can perform a protective function in respect of cognitive decline considered to be a high priority in view of the increasing incidence of dementia in later life as well as other mental disorders such as depression and anxiety. We believe that there is still some controversy concerning this broad claim, as we saw in the previous chapter, although the report subsequently considers a range of interventions that it is believed could help to improve mental capacity and boost well-being in later life. Among these is the promotion of social networking incorporating educational and social group interventions, although it is not clear what form these would take, and volunteering. From our perspective, a further suggested intervention – encouraging and enabling older people to engage with learning including initiatives that are designed to take account of their needs – is a positive suggestion, although we might question how these 'needs' would be identified and catered for in what we have seen is a highly diverse population. Older people's needs are, if anything, likely to be even more varied than those of younger people. A further recommendation, that of assisting older people to work if they wish, does appears to be a positive approach although it has to be pointed out that this would almost certainly require the government to review its current policy on the right to continue working. We return to this issue later in the chapter.

Another avenue explored is the exploitation of information and communications technology. As part of its potential role in assisting older people 'to remain socially and economically active for longer' this would hopefully offer new opportunities for learning, although this is something of a vague expectation unless it is to be accompanied by a sustained investment over a very long period. Those people in our study who were learning to use a computer focused only on understanding its operational procedures and did not comment on how they were planning to use it once they had mastered the necessary skills, although the possibilities have of course multiplied since our study was completed.

The authors of the report also stress that an important underlying requirement for their recommendations to work in practice is the need to address 'the stigma associated with older age' through an integrated approach that could involve 'teachers, families, the media, government and older people themselves' (Government Office for Science 2008: 36). Overall, it is suggested that older people could also be a key resource for planning and organizing any recommended interventions although it is not clear which older people would be involved. Such well-intentioned initiatives often fail to consult a representative sample of all older people in an area or region, not least because of the difficulties of making contact with older people who are not affiliated to any group or organization and encouraging them to take part. Considering how to locate our 'nonparticipants' was certainly an issue we faced at the beginning of our study and our solution would not necessarily be appropriate in other circumstances.

Whilst it would certainly be difficult to disagree with what are theoretically high ideals underpinning this part of the report, translating them into effective and lasting practice especially with a view to changing attitudes would be a lengthy and complex process. In the current economic climate in the UK, we have seen that lifelong learning now barely merits a reference within educational policy and, in any case, continues to lack any sound philosophy and, accordingly, an agreed strategic framework that would encompass its different dimensions including recognition of demographic trends. At present, the mechanisms for effecting such major changes are conspicuously lacking and, as we have seen, older people's access to learning opportunities has never been genuinely seen as a focus for educational investment. In view of the range of activities in which we have shown older people to be involved, what kind of learning opportunities would find favour and would they be adequately funded?

Indeed, there can be no cast-iron guarantee that the government will act upon on any of the recommendations within the report. However, it may be that, in combination with the outcomes of the current consultation on the future of non-vocational (informal) learning and the impact of different initiatives whose aim is to highlight the value and importance of lifelong learning as outlined in the previous chapter, a new concept of lifelong learning will emerge. Even so, we suspect that this may be little more than a return to a utopian 'cradle-to-grave' notion of what lifelong learning should entail, even if now justified by a better understanding of current social, economic and technological developments and couched in highly persuasive rhetoric. Any such vision would need to offer the potential for translation into policy terms and this may yet prove another stumbling block.

The contribution of our study

To continue this discussion, we now turn to a consideration of the contribution our study has made to thinking about lifelong learning in respect of what we have learnt concerning the choices older people make about learning in the light of their overall experiences. Obviously, it is important to allow for the time that has elapsed since our research was completed, as there are some new arguments to consider and the findings of subsequent projects that have examined similar questions to take into account.

From lifelong learning to longlife learning

We have discussed the various ways in which lifelong learning has been conceptualized and interpreted. We have shown that it has proved to be something of a moving target that has generated considerable rhetoric and has been used somewhat indiscriminately over the years to try to justify a range of different policies by a variety of sectoral interests at both international and national levels. Indeed, in spite of the challenges that the current Commission of Inquiry into the Future for Lifelong Learning has set itself, we now want to argue that the concept of lifelong learning has no future as such because constant change in society makes it almost impossible to devise an all-embracing framework within which different aspects could flourish over time. Overall, we are inclined to agree with those writers who have challenged the modernist stance of existing attempts to devise lifelong learning policies. Our model demonstrates that learning is an essentially individual undertaking; we need to understand it in terms of people's own interpretations of its meaning, their varied experiences of engagement with it at different levels and at different times, and their changing perceptions of its utility in their lives as they grow older. Accordingly, we should not make assumptions about older people's attitudes and levels of motivation to learn. Some people in our study reported positive early experiences that had encouraged them to see learning in a positive light throughout their lives. Yet we also saw that, even though some people had grown up in what seem to have been unfavourable circumstances and had had negative experiences of learning at school, they were largely able to overcome them over the life course and to look back and understand them within the context of the time.

Overall, we contend that, without a better grasp of the wide range of learning practices in which people, and older people in particular, are involved and a more finely nuanced understanding of what has influenced their choices and fuelled their aspirations, lifelong learning will continue to be little more than convenient rhetoric for disguising lack of action in making learning choices available or for ensuring optimum use of people's abilities and addressing their potential at any age. Any new vision will need to offer a more inclusive perspective in tune with many older people's beliefs that learning takes place right through life and is also life-wide, underpinned by stronger foundations and with an acknowledgement of the challenges that the implementation of such an approach will bring.

We believe that an alternative formulation might be to think in terms of 'longlife learning' that would straddle economic, democratic, personal and other concerns right across the life course in an inclusive way while foregrounding the undeniable impact of demographic trends. Learning in all its forms would then come to be seen as a more broadly based endeavour that incorporates the need for economic progress and social inclusiveness in tandem with recognition of individual desires for personal development and growth as people age. It would recognize that learning takes place in a range of everyday contexts as well as in a formal situation. Such learning need not necessarily be linear or even cumulative but it would be enduring and connective at a personal level. As such, it could offer a range of tangible benefits not just at individual but also at community and societal levels at different times. Indeed, it is worth recalling here the view of the focus group member who saw learning as being 'like ripples on a pond' in that it spreads out to all facets of life. This more pragmatic thinking partly echoes the views of Aspin and Chapman (2007) noted in our opening chapter and is in tune with the kind of debates advocated by Burke and Jackson (2007) in their own attempts to rethink and reconceptualize lifelong learning. However, in adopting a longlife learning perspective, it would still be necessary to take account of the ever-changing external context in which learning takes place as demonstrated within our model and to consider the longer-term impact of different developments and trends. Two examples, derived from our study, can be explored here.

Being post-work

Within our study, we chose not to make age itself a variable but used the term 'post-work' to refer to the situation of our study participants in the sense that they were no longer active in the labour market, at least on a full-time basis; and/or were no longer primarily concerned with raising a family even though many of our interviewees spent considerable time with children and grandchildren in the course of their daily lives. In other words, those who took part in our study were generally seen as 'retired'. However, in the light of current and future trends, it is now appropriate to re-examine use of this term.

We have already commented briefly on the gradual move away from traditional notions of retirement, especially in view of the UK government's plans to equalize the age for entry into the state pension scheme for men and women in 2010 and to raise it further to 68 in 2020. This means that many of the younger people now in the workforce will enter the post-work phase of life at a later age than is currently the case. As McNair (2007) pointed out, it is already government policy to encourage older people to stay for longer in employment in view of demographic trends that show fewer young people coming into the labour market and that fuel consequent fears about the growing dependency ratio.

A further recent development has been the implementation by the UK government and its devolved administrations of the age strand of the EU Employment Framework Directive (2000/78/EC). As interpreted by the government, this offers men and women the opportunity to request to continue working past the age of 65 yet, paradoxically, employers may still refuse this request without giving a reason. Indeed, a legal challenge to the UK interpretation of the legislation in the European Court of Justice mounted by the National Council on Ageing (operating under the names Age Concern and Heyday) has been unsuccessful. Certainly, in a difficult economic climate it is likely that many older employees will wish to continue working indefinitely in that they simply cannot afford to lose their income whilst others gain considerable enjoyment from the challenges their work provides and the comradeship it offers. Even if refused the chance to continue working in their current post, many people will seek out opportunities for part-time or other kinds of paid work, for self-employment or for fulfilling voluntary work as some of our study participants had already done. We have seen that, in the Foresight report, voluntary work is seen as having a useful function in the maintenance of well-being in later life, although we did not question our study participants on this issue. More evidence is needed regarding which aspects of continuing to work might ensure well-being, whatever the basis of older people's participation and the reasons underlying it.

Indeed, McNair points out that the transition from work into retirement has, in many cases, become more long drawn out as people choose to withdraw gradually or to take on new roles or activities once they have left full-time employment as discussed above. Hodkinson *et al.* (2008) also see retirement as a process, a lengthy transitional event that may include a series of changes over time although there may be a lack of clarity as to when it actually starts and finishes. Nevertheless, the authors suggest that, if we understand learning as a process of 'becoming', then learning, both formal and informal, is an inevitable and integral part of the process.

Denton and Spencer (2008), recognizing the extent to which retirement has become a problematic question, have reviewed and assessed the various concepts and measures that have been proposed in various countries to try to define it. They conclude that there are no straightforward definitions or measures available, but many of the examples they give reveal a very negative picture of retirement in that they give prominence to 'what people are not doing' (2008: 24) rather than including the wide range of other activities in which people participate and that may have considerable social value. Accordingly, they suggest that market-based measures should be complemented by a greater emphasis on understanding what people actually do, whether or not they might be officially classified as 'retired'. Meanwhile, Bolles and Nelson (2007), who specialize in retirement planning, suggest that the main question to be addressed should be 'what life will I retire *to*?' rather than 'what work will I retire *from*?' This is reflected in the philosophy of the UK Life Academy, whose work is based on the premise that life planning in all its forms should be a key focus of people's lives (www.life-academy.co.uk).

In view of these changes of perspective, it may no longer be adequate to categorize older people simply as those who are post-work. We have commented elsewhere on the difficulties of establishing exactly who we mean when we talk about older people, noting the range of prejudices and misconceptions that many people, including older people themselves, still sometimes hold about the processes of ageing (Withnall *et al.* 2004). Whilst the use of age-bands has now become an accepted way to explore and to try to understand the experiences of different cohorts, with age 50 frequently used as a base line, they note that various different agencies and government departments, especially those that collect educational data, use different criteria to establish who is 'older'.

Perhaps the most important point to remember when older people are under discussion is the range of age groups and variety of individual experiences that make up later life, as our study has shown even on a small scale. The need to respect and value individuality and diversity at any age and to recognize how our lives tend to diverge even further as we age has been consistently pointed out so that any assumption that older people are 'all the same' is both misguided and ageist (Withnall *et al.* 2004: 10). Taking labour market trends and subsequent policy changes into account, we would now argue that another important aspect of longlife learning is not just to include learning in what we termed the post-work period of life but also to address issues relating to learning for those who are still working in some capacity, however 'work' is interpreted.

Addressing frailty in later life

Not all older people want or are able to work. If we accept the need for inclusivity in thinking about later life, then we should also consider the very old and infirm in addition to the reasonably active older people on whom we mainly concentrated in our study. Although we were able to conduct one of our focus groups in a care home and there are emerging accounts of some admirable educational initiatives in different parts of the UK and elsewhere in Europe, it cannot be denied that both policy-makers and practitioners themselves have hitherto largely ignored older people in care settings and failed to consider their learning potential. A longlife approach would therefore need to explore the sense in which learning could be understood in such settings. In particular, it should consider how learning activities could be developed in respect of physically and mentally frail older people who require care and support, including those suffering from dementia and lesser degrees of cognitive impairment, and for whom connectivity would take on a different meaning. There is still a long way to go in this, although NIACE intends to revisit and reassess the current state of learning for people over 75, particularly those living in residential settings (Maltby 2008).

Even though it has to be acknowledged that frailty is not well defined or understood, Kitwood's philosophy of 'personhood' vested in relationships between carers and older people (Kitwood 1997) and the concept of 'wrap-around care' as a way of promoting well-being in dementia care (James 2008) might offer useful starting points. Nevertheless, the implications for training of managers, busy care staff and facilitators of learning, as well as the role of people caring for an elderly relative at home as some of our study participants were doing, are substantial. The National Association of Providers of Activities (NAPA) has made considerable progress in defining the issues to be addressed and devising workable strategies, but identifying adequate sources of funding through which the government could implement a national strategy is doubtless a major concern for the immediate future.

The life course approach

We have attempted to highlight and discuss our main empirical findings at each stage of our study, but it is worth commenting here on our overall approach. Through a focus on a growing sector of the population who, at the time our study was conceived, had been almost totally ignored in educational policy terms, we have drawn attention to some emerging theoretical perspectives on later life learning itself and made use of what was then an innovative life course approach to try to understand the kind of factors that influence older people's understanding of, and engagement with, learning post-work. Our methodology enabled a small group of older people to actively participate in the study and the voices of older people themselves to be heard at a time when there had been little research that attempted to move the focus of investigation to older learners themselves.

Biographical and life history methods of investigation have found favour in recent years in a range of studies both in education and in social gerontology as well as emerging as a tool for investigation in other aspects of social science. In our study, the use of a life course approach enabled the study participants to recall and give meaning to different aspects of their lives and to reflect on the role that learning has played in the past as well as how it impacts on their daily lives in retirement. It also assisted us in exploring the interplay of different factors as they affect people's lives and their learning activities, as our model demonstrates. In this sense, our study can claim to be innovative in that it succeeded in moving the focus of thinking about later life learning away from institutional concerns towards learners themselves. As we have said, however, the diversity of the older population and the sheer difficulties of disentangling the relative effects of different influences on individuals at different times proved to be a taxing and extremely complex task.

Within the TLRP, a much larger research project, *Learning Lives*, has since combined study of the learning biographies of a wider sample of adults aged 25–85 with an analysis of data from the British Household Panel Survey in order to identify some of the issues that affect learning through the life course. This study confirmed the extent to which people take part in learning throughout life and how involvement in learning often goes further than issues of participation. In some cases, learning was valued as an integral part of people's lives and bound up with their sense of identity, a finding that partially emerged in our own study. The research also uncovered a number of circumstances in which people particularly valued learning, largely confirming our own findings in respect of older people. As in our own study, these researchers further noted that learning can be enabled or, conversely, constrained by the situation in which individuals find themselves at any one time so that a range of strategies is required in order to meet different people's learning needs and circumstances at different times in their lives (Biesta 2008).

How can later life learning be improved?

On the basis of our findings and bearing in mind what we have said about the concept of longlife learning, we want to make some suggestions as to how later life learning might be improved in the interests of all adults as they grow older. In adding our views, we acknowledge the sterling work of the NIACE *Older and Bolder* programme over the last decade and the contribution of members of AEA to opening up debate. We also commend the comprehensive work of the charity Help the Aged, which has recently made an impassioned plea to government to recognize the kind of learning opportunities older people need to prevent them experiencing isolation and social exclusion (Help the Aged 2008a). Although we have commented on the fact that the idea of being 'post-work' no longer has the same connotations, for continuity we will address the issues in relation to people who see themselves as being primarily 'retired'. We believe that questions relating to learning for older people who continue to participate in the labour market past pensionable age or who undertake substantial amounts of voluntary work are of a different order and need to be very carefully framed and formulated. However, this does not preclude the fact that some of our comments will be relevant to adults of any age with a variety of lifestyles.

Implications for policy-makers

By sheer weight of numbers, older people are a force to be reckoned with. However, we are talking here about at least two different generations whose individual circumstances probably vary more than those of younger people, as do their life course experiences of learning and their attitudes towards it. We saw that many have been noticeably dismayed by the recent loss of courses and classes in some areas, as demonstrated in their responses to the government consultation on informal learning. A number of letters on the subject have also appeared in the educational press. Others, who would not anyway have considered taking part, may be involved in learning in a range of other ways or have a more holistic approach that sees them learning informally from their everyday lives and their social activities: these factors applied to many of the older people in our study. Older people in care settings have scarcely been considered at all. Yet we saw that later life learning has not just been promoted as an important facet of ageing well and healthily in a range of policy documents but is slowly being actively explored in various initiatives emanating from government departments other than DIUS. This suggests that there needs to be a better understanding between departments of the role of learning and a shared acceptance of the value it has in people's lives at any point in later life. The time has come to move on from well-intentioned rhetoric towards a better use of government resources and avoidance of duplication in the interests of all.

Both AEA and Help the Aged have stressed the need for a cross-governmental strategy to 'co-ordinate, monitor, promote and steer funding for learning opportunities' (Help the Aged 2008b: 6). They have also urged the DIUS to invest in a suitable infrastructure that would see such innovations as the appointment of a 'learning officer' or 'learning champion' in every locality, together with the availability of a learning portal and hard-copy directory of opportunities that embraces all possibilities for learning. Indeed, a multidisciplinary project conceived at the University of Warwick involved the development of an on-line toolkit powered by an intelligent software engine that could be used by learners to provide information and facilitate communication, but this sadly did not proceed beyond an initial exploration through lack of funding (Withnall 2007b).

We saw that some of our study participants were engaged in a range of both formal and informal learning activities at any one time whilst others dropped in and out of learning according to circumstances or had various ideas for activities they had considered at different times but had not followed up. Overall, it was apparent that many older people maintain or develop a variety of interests well into old age and enjoy learning in a range of different ways. Certainly, the easy availability of information as to what was available together with an indication of cost would have been useful to some of our study participants, who sometimes seemed to have relied on word of mouth as a source of knowledge about what they might do. However, we saw that some participants chose classes that they subsequently found to be unsatisfactory. The availability of accessible high-quality guidance services for older learners, the case for which has already been strenuously argued by Ford (2005), might go some way to assisting older people in making appropriate choices as to the type of learning they would enjoy. We believe that older learners, even if learning informally, need more support to develop their interests in the context of their beliefs about the overall benefits of learning. An extension of the Information, Advice and Guidance (IAG) Service to include all older people, not just those still active in the labour market, would pay dividends in helping older people to follow up their interests. It could also help them to be more aware of ways in which they could continue making a contribution to their communities through sharing their interests with others or taking up a volunteer role whatever their age and circumstances.

We saw that a few of our study participants had completed degrees or other accredited courses since retiring and others were enjoying the intellectual challenge of formal study either through a college course or through membership of the University of the Third Age. Another had vaguely considered the possibilities of the Open University. Attending lectures and musical events and visiting museums and galleries were also part of some respondents' lives. We also noted that those of our respondents who lived in some form of sheltered housing enjoyed the company and range of activities on offer in a safe environment as well as continuing with their own interests outside their community. Indeed, recent years have seen a considerable expansion in the development of private housing developments for retired people together with the growth of 'retirement villages' often with superb social facilities that offer the space for developing residents' various interests. There are considerable possibilities here for stronger policies in relation to the development of retirement and extra care communities which the Department of Health has begun to consider initially through the work of its Housing Learning and Improvement Network (DH 2004).

In the USA, the concept of the university-based retirement community has witnessed a substantial growth in recent years. Although there is no one model, the guiding principle is that older people are enabled to live safely and independently among like-minded peers in an educational community with access to classes and courses and to all the facilities that a university campus offers. An added bonus is intergenerational interaction with students, academics and administrative staff who can also be challenged to face up to any negative attitudes to ageing they may hold. Many of the American models strive to offer the full range of housing services for older people so that residents are not forced to move if they become physically and mentally frail and require more skilled nursing care (Larkin 2007). Obviously, with current government emphasis on widening participation for 18–30-year-olds in higher education in the UK, universities and colleges are unlikely to see the benefits of developing campus-based retirement communities in the short term; and it has to be recognized that, even with private sponsorship, such developments would be expensive both for institutions and for older residents themselves. However, as the birthrate continues to fall, some of the larger campus-based universities may yet come to welcome older students and to consider developing innovative programmes for them (Gordon and Shinagel 2004). Older people represent a largely untapped market, especially as successive cohorts who have been exposed to better educational opportunities move into later life.

Of course, residence on a university campus is not for everyone. Our study also revealed a few examples of older men who led fairly solitary lives together with a number of women on their own who, whilst currently enjoying good social lives in which learning played a part, may not continue to do so as they grow older. We also saw others who enjoyed learning as a couple; but, as people aged, their learning interests and hobbies necessarily became more home-based and the media, especially television, became an important stimulus to developing new learning interests. Some years ago, the Department of Continuing Education at Lancaster University developed an innovative *Learning From Home* programme that enabled groups of adults, many of whom were older people living in rural areas, to take part in telephone conference discussions around books they had read or television programmes they had enjoyed together with what was then an early experiment in on-line discussion for those exploring the possibilities offered by information technology. Some U3A groups have experimented along similar lines. In addition, the growing popularity of book groups in the UK suggests that this might be another useful and cost-effective way of helping older people get together with others in a community or library venue or even in people's homes. Neuberger (2008) believes that Neighbourhood Watch organizations could have a role to play here in identifying isolated older people and inviting them to participate in some kind of group activity as well as linking with other relevant local organizations such as Age Concern. However, we are in agreement with Help the Aged's argument that local authorities should each develop an Older People's Strategy that could incorporate increased opportunities for learning through which older people could be 'signposted' towards activities that are appropriate for their own situation.

In putting forward these suggestions, we acknowledge that not all older people want to learn solely in the company of other older people. Some of our study participants chose to learn in a range of different situations, including more conventional courses in the company of people of all ages. It is to be hoped that any future government lifelong learning strategies will acknowledge how important access to these kinds of opportunities is for many older people and will ensure that affordable formal education and training classes and courses are still available for those who prefer the stimulus of learning in this way. Although increasingly popular, the kind of self-help learning developed in the U3A model is not appropriate for everyone.

Implications for practitioners

It is constantly stressed that older people are not a homogeneous group and, on a small scale, our study has illustrated well the many differences in their backgrounds and current circumstances as well as in their daily activities, interests and abilities. Yet the different contextual and personal factors that have impacted on their lives, their experiences of engagement with learning over the life course and their individual motivations and aspirations in retirement are rarely taken into account when learning activities are being planned, whether this is by professional educators or by facilitators including older people teaching their peers. We suggest that people's very different experiences of education and beliefs about learning need to be considered much more carefully in the design of teaching, learning and training programmes, whatever the level. This includes activities that are specifically aimed at older people and those intended for mixed-age groups wherever they are held.

In particular, we observed that older people may drop in and out of learning according to their personal circumstances. Therefore, any publicity needs to be carefully designed so that potential learners know exactly what is being offered and at what level, especially if they have been away from learning for some time. This seemed to be particularly relevant for those embarking on learning a language or a more practical skill. Our findings also suggest that, rather than analysing the barriers that are said to militate against older people's participation, it would be more productive if practitioners were to concentrate on identifying the factors that do encourage them to take part. These include recognition of the point in retirement when older people are ready to try something new; between three and ten years after retirement appeared to be the optimum time for our learners. Another factor was the importance of having someone to accompany them to an activity whatever the setting. Some people enjoyed going along with a spouse of friend even if not involved in the same activity whilst some of the women in one of the focus groups remarked on the necessity of having someone to accompany them home and to see them safely into the house. Members of another focus group were collected and taken home by minibus and, whilst this is an ideal solution, it is likely to be costly.

Even among those who did not initially see themselves as current learners, it was apparent that many of our study participants were actually engaging in learning in a range of social and other situations. We are in agreement with Biesta (2008) who, as part of the TLRP *Learning Lives* project, noted the ways in which the 'learning culture' in such situations can be enhanced, stressing that this must always be pragmatic. Certainly, as was revealed in some of our interview data, membership of, for example, various different clubs and local societies offered considerable opportunities for members to learn. If they could be helped both to recognize this and to share their knowledge and skills with peers and with other generations, these benefits of learning would have a wider effect, especially in rural or other areas where more formal learning opportunities are necessarily restricted.

Indeed, our findings also demonstrate the importance of self-organized and incidental learning in older people's lives even if they are already learning formally or plan to do so. Our interviewees were found to make use of a variety of sources to follow up interests and hobbies to a greater extent than was previously realized but they were largely reliant on identifying these sources themselves. Practitioners could assist here by ensuring that a wider range of resources, such as those produced by the BBC and independent television companies, and sources of support are made more visible and more readily available to lone learners. Broadcasting companies themselves would also benefit from a better understanding of older adults' learning interests. Such levels of personal support have been found to be especially relevant to older people trying to organize a learning project for themselves in rural areas (Roberson and Merriam 2005).

Further research

We have acknowledged elsewhere that, overall, the research that has been carried out in respect of later life learning is highly fragmented and usually small-scale (Withnall 2008). A more recent review of the literature carried out for the AEA came to much the same conclusion and added that 'the connections between research, practice and policy . . . do not appear to be well made' (Anderson 2008: 55). Accordingly, we believe that almost every aspect of later life learning would benefit from more rigorous well-funded investigation and evaluation. We would especially like to see more longitudinal studies that track older learners over a period of time together with a more focused exploration of how older people themselves could participate meaningfully in educational research. However, on the basis of our study, we want to draw attention to what we see as some immediate gaps in our knowledge.

For almost everyone in our study, learning in its different forms played an important part in their daily lives, especially as we uncovered what appears to be the very large amount of informal learning taking place in later life. Certainly, we need a better understanding of the ways in which older people learn, whether and how they differ from the methods used by younger people and, if so, how their learning could be enhanced across a whole range of settings. This is particularly important because older people could also be given far more formal encouragement to share their knowledge and skills with other generations (not just children) and to learn from them in return. We saw that the intergenerational movement is gathering impetus worldwide and the initiatives set up in Wales and Scotland have at least begun to recognize the value of this approach within the UK.

Although we touched upon it in the original project, we did not explore here the impact of the costs associated with different types of learning for different groups of older people to any extent. Costs would not just include fees for classes and courses but would incorporate the additional expense of, for example, books, materials and computers together with any travel costs both to a venue and for learning-related visits and other activities. There is very little research that has systematically investigated what different groups of older people are prepared to pay for their learning but the popularity of U3A and the amount of informal learning taking place suggests that low cost is a major factor influencing people's choices about learning. In a time of economic recession, it would be useful to further explore older people's attitudes to this issue. In addition, we need robust financial information concerning the cost of developing learning opportunities in care settings before any policy decisions are made.

We have seen that much of the learning in which our study participants were involved and its outcomes for their lives, their communities and society in general were hidden because they were not accredited. Some years ago, Withnall and Percy (1994) advocated encouraging the visibility of older adults in a whole range of educational contexts partly as a way of challenging prevailing negative stereotypes of older people and their capabilities. Since our study was completed, a small but growing number of festivals, performances, exhibitions and competitions that showcase the products and outcomes of older people's learning, including their involvement in the arts, have begun to appear. There is a need to explore the overall impact of such events and their potential for attracting older people to learning in all its forms.

Finally, we want to acknowledge that our study has provided what we described as a snapshot in time of the experiences of a relatively small number of older people, most of whom lived through the Second World War or at least experienced some of the privations of its aftermath. People now moving into later life grew up in rather different circumstances, and the experiences and expectations of subsequent cohorts will doubtless provide some additional new challenges. We believe the model developed in this study can be adapted and expanded to incorporate the march of time, the changing balance of influences on people's propensity to learn in later life and the outcomes learning has for their lives. In particular, as information and communications technology continues to develop at an astonishing pace, a whole new range of learning methodologies are becoming available; now and in the future older people should be helped to make use of these in the same way that younger people take for granted.

Conclusion

In this chapter, we have suggested that, in view of demographic trends and the difficulties inherent in understanding lifelong learning in any meaningful way, we adopt the concept of 'longlife learning'. We believe that this kind of thinking would help us to move towards a more inclusive society where all forms of learning are valued, older people are held in higher esteem for the visible contribution they make to society and learning for everyone is truly acknowledged as a desirable process relevant to the reality of long life. Above all, we want to emphasize that people's learning, whatever form it takes, is located in a constantly changing external context that impacts throughout life on individual experiences and beliefs and continues to do so as people age. It is an issue that concerns us all; no one is immune to growing older.

How the research was carried out

Introduction

The research was conducted over a period of thirty months between 2000 and 2002 with a research team originally consisting of the Principal Investigator and a full-time Research Fellow joined temporarily by an interviewing team of older people themselves as described below. Because of the time that has elapsed since the study was carried out, it has been important to reconsider the processes and findings of the research within the current political and socio-economic climate and with reference to more recent publications relating to later life learning as interest in older people's access to educational opportunities has grown in different countries. The inclusion of the study as an associated project within the ESRC *Teaching and Learning Research Programme* has also afforded a new opportunity to reconsider the findings in relation to other project findings in education, especially in relation to the theme of lifelong learning, rather than as an issue to be discussed solely in relation to the ageing of the population.

Ethical issues

At the time it was devised, the study was not subject to approval by an Ethics Committee. However, the research was informed at all stages by the Code of Conduct, Ethical Principles and Guidelines produced by the British Psychological Society (1997). In particular, attention was paid to issues of (1) honesty to research staff, fieldworkers and Project Consultants concerning the purposes, methods and intended and possible uses of the research; (2) gaining informed consent from all research participants including those who may have had age-related impairments; (3) the right of withdrawal from the study at any time; (4) confidentiality and anonymity of research participant; (5) boundaries on privacy and self-disclosure in any focus group discussions; and (6) the responsibility of investigators for ethical treatment of research participants. The ways in which these requirements were to be addressed in the study were detailed within the original bid to the ESRC. In addition, although the requirements of the Data Protection

Act (2001) were not yet in force, care was given to approach potential participants through a 'gatekeeper' where possible; all research material had any identifying features removed during preparation for archiving.

Research methods

At the outset, a mainly qualitative approach, chosen for its capacity to produce rich data and for its attention to complexity and process (Sankar and Gubrium 1994) was seen as the most appropriate form of enquiry. It was intended that the approaches adopted would ensure that members of the research team would be able to take a critical stance towards the research at all stages and would give consideration to how the research findings were written, presented and disseminated through feedback to research subjects, checks on validity and invitations to comment. Additionally, an important aspect of the study was to develop research strategies that would draw on a variety of investigative techniques. In accordance with the stated aim of maximizing the participation of older people themselves in the research, it was planned to involve a small team of older people to carry out the interviews in this stage of the research. It was assumed that use of peer interviewers would be a positive step in that older people are more likely to be able to share at least some of the interviewees' perspectives; and their inclusion might help to avoid any mutual misunderstandings in discussion and in language used.

In retrospect, this may have been a rather simplistic view. At the time the study was designed, there were few examples of this kind of involvement but, as Dewar (2005) has since argued from a health and social care perspective, assumptions commonly made about the involvement of older people in the research process probably need to be challenged. For example, she believes it is important to move beyond anecdotal accounts in order to be more critical of why it is important to involve older people at all. She also wonders whether the knowledge generated through such involvement can be more 'authentic' and suggests that further work is required to explore the kind of education that could prepare older people to work in an equal partnership with researchers whilst recognizing that their contribution is of a different order. More recently, Barnes and Taylor (2007) have considered the various ways in which older people have now participated in different kinds of research and have produced a good practice guide to involving older people at every stage. Although most of the processes we adopted in our own study did comply with their subsequent recommendations, in retrospect it might have been appropriate to invite some of our research participants to comment more fully on the findings as the study progressed, especially in relation to the interviews. Time constraints made it difficult to fulfil this aim to the extent that had originally been intended.

The research was carried out in overlapping stages over the thirty-month period. The methods adopted, reasons for their choice and the issues that arose and that may have implications for other researchers are discussed in more detail below.

Stage 1

A comprehensive literature review of what was known about later life learning had already been carried out as part of the original bid made to the ESRC under the *Growing Older: Extending Quality Life Programme* (2000–2004). In the first stage of the project, this was revised where necessary and has since been considerably updated to take into account findings and viewpoints from more recent studies, especially in view of the development of the literature of lifelong learning.

While the initial revision of the literature review was under way, recruitment commenced of a team of older people to act as interviewers in Stage 4 of the study. Targeted publicity in a local evening paper together with an interview on a local radio station resulted in a number of telephone calls and letters from interested older people living locally although some subsequently decided not to proceed on learning what was involved. Other potential interviewers in different parts of the country were recruited with help from the two Project Consultants and from different older people's organizations. Further details of the team and how its members operated are given below (Stage 4). During this stage, consideration was also given as to how to locate and organize potential focus group participants for the next phase of the study.

Stage 2

In locating relevant groups of learners, use was made of the original Mapping Tool produced by the UK Secretariat for the International Year of Older People (Soulsby 2000) as a sampling frame. This consists of an extensive list of categories of organizations that may provide older people with opportunities for learning in some form including training for a specific volunteer role. Initially, however, those categories where the organizations did not specifically have the provision of learning opportunities as a prime focus were eliminated. Within the remaining categories, the research team located and approached a contact name across a range of organizations using a specially designed recruitment flyer. This gave details of the proposed focus groups along with assurances of anonymity and confidentiality. That there was no requirement for potential participants to reveal their ages was also stressed. More general information about the overall purpose of the research and an introduction to the research team members were included separately. Agreement to participate was eventually obtained from ten groups. Each group was from a different category with the widest possible geographical spread (England, Scotland, Wales) and representing a whole variety of activities including, in one case, those organized by older people themselves. One group was composed entirely of ethnic minority members and one was based within a residential home. Not all members of the individual focus groups were learning together but, in every group, everyone knew the others at some level. It was considered that the number of focus groups chosen would generate adequate data for research purposes although little agreement exists as to whether there can be an optimum number of groups in focus-group-based research (McLafferty 2004).

Two additional points may be made here in relation to the recruitment process. Firstly, in locating groups of older learners prepared to give up time to participate, the research team was sometimes made very aware of the role of 'gatekeepers', often younger professionals who displayed a particularly protective concern with regard to the older people in the organizations in which they worked. However, in all cases, there was considerable interest in taking part among the older learners themselves once the gatekeeper had been persuaded to allow access. Members of the organization run by older people themselves were also keen to participate in order that their views could be heard. It may be that more preliminary work with gatekeepers to explain the benefits to older people of encouraging them to take part and the use of payment to participants together with more emphasis on ethical issues of confidentiality would have helped to overcome the difficulties experienced.

Secondly, as an experiment a trustworthy e-organization for older people was contacted and its agreement received to host an e-focus group discussion. Information about the overall study and the purpose of the focus group was advertised on the notice board in the organization's Learning Curve Room that was specifically dedicated to chat about learning issues. Members of the e-organization were not required to sign up in advance for the focus group and consent was not sought in advance. The discussion was advertised for a specific day and time in order for a researcher to be in the Chat Room and to maximize the potential for group discussion. Questions for discussion were to be posted in the Learning Curve foyer, the first site learners encounter when they enter the Learning Curve Room. The focus group discussion was to be logged by the e-organization (as are all exchanges in the Chat Rooms) and a text copy provided for analysis.

In the event, no one entered the Chat Room during the time allotted for the focus group discussion. It was concluded that possible participants did not yet feel sufficiently confident to discuss personal histories and opinions in on-line debate, although timing may also have been an issue. Spending time in the Chat Room prior to the proposed discussion and actively recruiting participants to join in at the allotted time together with emphasis on ensuring confidentiality might have proved a more effective way of encouraging participation. Certainly this method has the potential to access the increasing number of older people who are computer-literate, whether or not they engage with other learning activities, and could prove to be a useful research tool in future, providing ethical issues can be addressed beforehand.

Questions designed to stimulate debate among focus group participants must be carefully formulated. As Chioncel *et al.* (2003) have confirmed, lack of precision and consistency can threaten the internal validity of focus groups. At the same time, the research team wanted to allow for the groups to lead the discussion in new directions (Field 2000) if appropriate and to be able to hear any dissenting voices. Initially, a broad list of possible questions was drawn up and was then refined in further discussion and incorporated into an interview guide. This consisted of six main questions moving from those initially aimed at obtaining a picture of historical events and changes in society that participants might perceive to have affected their lives to more focused questions designed to encourage reflection on their learning experiences as children, as adults and, additionally, in the post-work period. Accordingly, a subset to each question, which could be used to stimulate and focus discussion while allowing for participants to raise their own issues where necessary, was also devised. The questions were piloted with two older people known personally to research team members to ensure that they were clearly formulated, could be readily understood and would encourage reflection.

The interview questions were incorporated into a field note reporting form for each focus group, which allowed a researcher acting as moderator to make notes of the main points of the discussion together with additional observations and relevant details that were added either at the time or after due reflection. Focus group participants were not aware of the exact questions in advance as it was felt that this would militate against spontaneous discussion.

In organizing and conducting the discussions, the research team followed the practical guidelines suggested by Quine (1998) based largely on her own experiences of conducting focus groups with older people who may have some degree of age-related physical or sensory impairment. Each focus group took place on the premises of the organization in which it was based. Awareness of the possible impact of different contexts on the data collected (Green and Hart 1999) meant that care was taken in each case to provide a comfortable and familiar venue where participants could feel relaxed and where seating arrangements enabled them to talk to each other and to the moderator without feeling constrained.

Details of how ethical issues were addressed in practice, the discussions within the focus groups, analysis of data and the findings are discussed in detail in Part 2, Chapter 3. As described, one of the outcomes of the focus group discussions was intended to be a conceptual model of older people's lifetime encounters with education and learning and the influences on it based on participants' perceptions and interpretations of their own experiences. The research team devised several versions of a possible model at the conclusion of this stage of the study; that finally chosen allowed for possible revision and expansion in later stages of the research.

Stage 3

The main aim in this stage was to test and refine the model if necessary by enabling two larger and more diverse groups of older people, one of whom would not necessarily be currently involved in learning, to reflect on their life course experiences and understandings of learning through a mailed questionnaire using a partially open-ended format. The basic question-naires were piloted with two older people known to the research team to ensure that they were clear. On the basis of their comments some alter-ations were made to the wording of some of the questions and spacing between the questions was revised. The questionnaires were then produced in an attractive booklet format with an indication of the estimated time taken to complete them and with clear symbols for navigation through the pages since not all the questions were relevant for both groups of respon-dents.

In locating potential questionnaire respondents who were currently taking part in a course or class of some kind, use was again made of the Mapping Tool (Soulsby 2000) to select ten sites different from those chosen for the focus groups. This time, organizations that were not necessarily educational in focus but which did incorporate learning opportunities in their activities were included. However, locating suitable organizations and persuading them to participate in the study proved particularly difficult and time-consuming; once again, some gatekeepers were anxious to protect their members' interests. The assistance of the Project Consultants with their extensive range of contacts was instrumental in helping the research team gain access in this respect. In addition, the co-operation of different members of the Association for Education and Ageing (AEA) who freely offered advice and help must also be acknowledged.

The sampling frame for this stage of the research was intended to consist of all registered members of each organization from whom fifty (five at each site) would be chosen to receive a questionnaire using systematic selection. In the event, because it was not always possible for the research team to access this information, reliance sometimes had to be placed on the co-operation of gatekeepers or Project Consultants to undertake selection after the desired method had been explained. This was not ideal but all those asked co-operated fully and appear to have undertaken selection with diligence and care reflected in the high number of older people who agreed to participate in the study at this stage.

As stated, a further aim of this stage of the study was to make contact with an equivalent number of older people who did not appear to be currently involved in any kind of formally organized learning activity in order to also investigate their backgrounds and perceptions of learning. It was accepted that they may nevertheless have been undertaking other kinds of formal or informally based learning according to their own understanding of what learning actually entails. To identify such a group of older people, use was therefore made of a snowballing technique whereby each original questionnaire respondent was also asked to supply contact details, with the individual's permission, of an older person they knew who was not currently participating in a class or course and who would be willing to take part in the study. It was recognized that this is an uncertain and contingent process and that results must be interpreted with caution, but it was felt that it was an acceptable technique in what was a largely exploratory study. To minimize non-response, details of the study were supplied to each potential respondent in advance and their co-operation formally sought before the questionnaires were dispatched. This included an explanation of how responses would be analysed and by whom and where the information would be stored.

With the questionnaire, respondents received a covering letter thanking them for taking part and containing instructions for questionnaire completion and return including a pre-paid envelope. Potential recipients were not required to give their names or ages, although many subsequently did so, and respondents were identified only by a number. They were asked separately to give permission for archiving of the material as required by the ESRC; however, for reasons that were not completely clear, a majority subsequently refused. It may be that in spite of assurances of anonymity, they had concerns over who would have access to the material once it was archived and the use that would be made of it. They were also asked whether they would be willing to take part in a further stage of the research. It was explained that this would take the form of an in-depth interview or a request to keep a learning 'log' or diary over a period of three months although it was stressed that some respondents would not necessarily be selected for further involvement.

One hundred questionnaires (fifty to 'participants' and fifty to 'nonparticipants') were sent out in all. As discussed in Chapter 4, an overall response rate of 77 per cent was obtained. As both questionnaires were fairly long and detailed, and, it was estimated, would take around forty minutes to complete, this was a surprisingly high rate. It appears that careful planning and targeting of potential respondents was a factor in this success. However, some of the respondents, whether current learners or not, commented on how pleased they were that they had been asked for their views and that the research team had shown interest in their lives. The questionnaires were originally analysed using both SPSS for Windows and thematic analysis for the open-ended questions. However, recent re-analysis of the questionnaires revealed that some of the original questions, such as those relating to the current financial costs of joining a course or class, were no longer relevant since information supplied in the responses is now out of date. Other questions, especially those relating to

respondents' early lives, produced a surfeit of sometimes irrelevant information and were omitted from the overall analysis.

The data obtained via the questionnaires would allow for refinement of
the conceptual model if appropriate although, as noted in Chapter 6, this
proved to be unnecessary.

Stage 4

As discussed in Chapter 5 and detailed above, the questionnaires were to
be supplemented by semi-structured interviews. From the names of those
who had agreed to this, alternate names were selected, with the interviews
to be carried out by a team of older people themselves. Accordingly, eight
older people, four men and four women, located in different parts of the
country and ranging in age from 59 to 76, were recruited to act as paid
interviewers although one woman subsequently withdrew following
spousal bereavement. Clear criteria were specified for the role and interviewers were made aware of the overall time commitment that would be
needed. They were employed on a casual basis by the University where the
research was based and were asked to carry out five interviews each as near
to their homes as possible for which they were offered a generous one-off
fee to include travel and subsistence. The University also provided insur-
ance cover and some advice on the tax implications of casual employment
in retirement for those likely to be affected. Interview dates and times were
arranged by a member of the research team at mutually convenient times
either in the interviewee's own home or in a public venue where preferred;
both interviewers and interviewees were given comprehensive advice on
personal safety issues. Interviewers were provided with official identification, a good-quality tape recorder and tapes and a fieldwork report form
on which to record their own impressions of the interview immediately
afterwards. They were also supplied with pre-paid packaging in which to
return tapes, equipment and fieldwork report forms.

Leamy and Clough (2006) have described how a group of older people
were offered the opportunity to study for a university-accredited Certificate
in Social Research Methods for Older People in order to equip them both
with a theoretical understanding of research and with practical interviewing skills so that they were able to play an active part in a major three-year
research project on housing decisions in later life. In our study, it had
originally been intended to run a series of face-to-face training days for the
interviewers in different parts of the country to help them with the interviewing process, although most were confident in their abilities, often as a
result of previous experience gained in the workplace or in the voluntary
sector. In any case, because of time constraints and cost restrictions, it
would not have been possible to provide the kind of training described in
Leamy and Clough's report. Eventually, a decision was taken instead to produce a training manual for each interviewer along with the list of possible

questions. The manual contained clear advice on active listening skills and on developing openness and empathy with the interviewee as well as help on avoiding leading or loaded questions. Simple advice on how to operate the equipment was also included. Interviewers were required to sign a form to the effect that they understood the need for confidentiality at all stages and were also provided with a contact telephone number if any problems arose.

To a great extent, trust was an important element in the interview process in that considerable reliance was placed on the willingness and ability of members of the interview team to study and absorb the guidance given and to establish rapport with the interviewees in such a way that the objectives of the interview could be achieved. Based in England, Wales and Northern Ireland, interviewers were matched as far as possible with interviewees taking into account the need to avoid lengthy travelling times but all had the chance to interview participants and non-participants and both men and women. Interviews generally lasted for between one and two hours with permission to record the interview again being sought at the outset. It is worth noting here that, although the arrangements were time-consuming to set up, they appeared to have been greatly appreciated by the interview team and to have given them the confidence to conduct the interviews in a professional manner.

A semi-structured interview format was chosen because it offered the opportunity for interviewers to guide the interaction and to maintain a focus on the specific topics to be investigated while also allowing for a deeper and richer understanding of interviewees' perspectives on their lives and on learning to emerge. Two interview schedules were devised and piloted since it was obviously necessary to vary the questions for the two groups; where participants were invited to reflect on their current learning activity, non-participants were asked whether they had considered any learning activity since retiring and if so, to reflect on why they had not pursued it as well as indicating any future intentions to learn.

All the interviews were transcribed verbatim and each was read initially in conjunction with the relevant field notes not only to gain an overview of each interviewee's perspective but also to provide a sense of the process of the individual interviews and the way in which emergent topics were raised and discussed. Where necessary, the interviewees' self-reports of their current living arrangements and any learning activities were checked against information given in their earlier questionnaire responses to ensure validity. Transcripts were then analysed thematically. This procedure involved several readings of the transcripts to identify and note recurrent themes and topics and the frequency with which they occurred as well as being alert to repeated statements and strongly expressed views throughout (Luborsky 1994). The transcriber, herself recently retired, also completed notes on her experiences of listening to the tapes so that comments on any difficulties she experienced in producing transcripts could be addressed and additional advice incorporated into a new version of the interviewers' guide for potential use in other projects.

A large-print learning 'log' in the form of a diary was also designed to enable a further group of older people to record their involvement and experiences of any learning activity, as defined by the diarists themselves. The diary was designed in A4 format using large print and with clear instructions for completion and return. The aim was to allow for a fairly simple coding of activities by the research team. Accordingly, twenty of the people (ten of each gender) who had filled out questionnaires and had expressed interest in further involvement were also selected at random and agreed to take part. The logs were to be analysed to identify the amount and types of learning activity that these older people reported undertaking. However, it must be acknowledged that asking people to log their activities for use as a research tool is somewhat risky since it assumes the ability to remember to complete it accurately on a daily basis, to be able to recall and describe activities, to reflect on and to categorize them and, of course, it also requires a fairly high degree of literacy as well as the simple ability to hold a pen. This in itself may be a problem for an older person suffering from, for example, arthritis in the fingers. Others may have sight problems that make concentration difficult, while some potential diarists may have been embarrassed by the knowledge that both their writing ability and their daily activities would be subject to scrutiny by others. With hindsight, it might have been easier and more practical to have invited the older people concerned to record their experiences on tape and to add their own comments on how they felt about the experience. Some other types of difficulties encountered in conducting diary-based research have since been discussed in detail by Bytheway and Johnson (2002), who nevertheless regard it as having considerable potential as a way of understanding, for example, the positive interchange that can take place between older people and their communities.

Stage 5

The last part of the project involved the preparation of a final report using biographical analysis for a framework. When this was complete, a professionally printed summary of the study and the findings was produced in a brochure format. Attractively illustrated and addressed to everyone who had had any kind of involvement in the research, it was sent out as a 'thank you' gesture and with an invitation to comment. Informal feedback suggested that many of those who had taken part in focus groups or had been interviewed had enjoyed the experience of talking about their lives and some had subsequently decided to explore what other learning opportunities were available in their area, with particular interest in the possibilities of the University of the Third Age. Some of the interviewers also reported considerable satisfaction with the experience, especially enhanced confidence in their own communication skills. One had donated most of her fee to the older people's group she herself attended to help purchase a new computer that would be of wider benefit to group members.

The future

Participation in the TLRP allowed for retrospective reflection on the methods adopted in the original study and some evaluation of how successful they had been in the light of more recent work with older people. Whilst this was a comparatively small study, we believe it has opened the way for more creative thinking about ways of investigating older people's engagement with learning. We hope others will draw inspiration from our approach and that more sophisticated studies in which older learners themselves can participate on an equal footing will continue to inform our understanding.

References

Ahl, H. (2006) 'Motivation in adult education: a problem solver or a euphemism for direction and control?' *International Journal of Lifelong Education*, 25: 385–405.

Aldridge, F. and Tuckett, A. (2007) *What Older People Learn*, Leicester: NIACE.

Allman, P. (1984) 'Self-help learning and its relevance for learning and development in later life', in E. Midwinter (ed.) *Mutual Aid Universities*, London: Croom Helm.

Anderson, S. (2008) *Later Life Learning: A Review of the Literature*, unpublished report, London: Association for Education and Ageing. Online. Available HTTP: http://www.cpa.org (accessed 2 July 2008).

Aspin, D. and Chapman, J.D. (eds) (2007) 'Lifelong learning: concepts and conceptions', in D. Aspin (ed.) *Philosophical Perspectives on Lifelong Learning*, Dordrecht: Springer.

Audit Commission (2008) *Don't Stop Me Now. Preparing for an Ageing Population*, Local Government National Report, London: Audit Commission.

Barnes, M. and Taylor, S. (2007) *Good Practice Guide. Involving Older People in Research: Examples, Purposes and Good Practice*. Online. Available HTTP: http://www.shef.ac.uk/era-age (accessed 1 October 2007).

Battersby, D. (1986) 'The "Third Age" revolution on Australasian campuses: the question', *Journal of Educational Gerontology*, 1: 8–16.

Battersby, D. (1987) 'From andragogy to geragogy', *Journal of Educational Gerontology*, 2: 4–10.

Battersby, D. (1993) 'Developing an epistemology of professional practice within educational gerontology', *Journal of Educational Gerontology*, 8: 17–25.

Beddington, J., Cooper, C.L., Field, J., Goswami, U., Huppert, F.A., Jenkins, R., Jones, H.S., Kirkwood, T.B.L., Sahakian, B.J., and Thomas, S.M. (2008) 'The mental wealth of nations', *Nature*, 455: 1057–60.

Bergeman, C.S. (1997) *Aging. Genetic and Environmental Influences*, Thousand Oaks, CA: Sage Publications.

Biesta, G. (2008) *Strategies for Improving Learning Through the Life-Course*, London: TLRP.

Blaikie, A. (1999) *Ageing and Popular Culture*, Cambridge: Cambridge University Press.

Bolles, R.N. and Nelson, J.E. (2007) *What Color Is Your Parachute? For Retirement*, Berkeley, CA: Ten Speed Press.

Brine, J. (2006) 'Lifelong learning and the knowledge economy: those that know and those who do not – the discourse of the European Union', *British Educational Research Journal*, 32: 649–65.

British Psychological Society (1997) *Code of Conduct, Ethical Principles and Guidelines*, Leicester: BPS.

Bunyan, K. and Jordan, A. (2005) 'Too late for the learning: lessons from older learners', *Research in Post-Compulsory Education*, 10: 267–81.

Burke, P.J. and Jackson, S. (2007) *Reconceptualising Lifelong Learning. Feminist Interventions*, Abingdon: Routledge.

Bytheway, B. (ed.) (2003) *Everyday Living in Later Life*, London: Centre for Ageing and Biographical Studies, the Open University and the Centre for Policy on Ageing.

Bytheway, B. and Johnson, J. (2002) 'Doing diary-based research', in A. Jamieson and C.R.Victor (eds) *Researching Ageing and Later Life*, Buckingham: Open University Press.

Carlton, S. and Soulsby, J. (1999) *Learning to Grow Older and Bolder*, Leicester: NIACE.

Central Office of Information (2008) *Informal Adult Learning – Shaping the Way Ahead. Consultation Response Analysis Report*, London: Department for Innovation, Universities and Skills.

Chioncel, N.E., Van der Veen, R.G.W., Wildermeersch D. and Jarvis, P. (2003) 'The value and reliability of focus groups as a research method in adult education', *International Journal of Lifelong Education*, 22: 495–517.

Chiu, L.-F. and Knight, D. (1999) 'How useful are focus groups for obtaining the views of minority groups?', in R.S. Barbour and J. Kitzinger (eds) *Developing Focus Group Research*, London: Sage Publications.

Coffield, F. (2008) 'When the problem is the solution . . .', *UC Magazine*, October: 9–10.

Cohen, G.D. (2005) *The Mature Mind. The Positive Power of the Aging Brain*, New York, NY: Basic Books.

Cusack, S. (1999) 'Critical educational gerontology and the imperative to empower', *Educational Gerontology*, 14: 21–37.

De Medeiros, K., Harris-Trovato, D., Bradley, E., Gaines, J. and Parrish, J. (2007) 'Group dynamics in a discussion group for older adults: does gender play a role?', *Educational Gerontology*, 33: 111–25.

Deakin Crick, R. and Wilson, K. (2005) 'Being a learner: a virtue for the 21st Century', *British Journal of Educational Studies*, 53: 359–74.

Dehmel, A. (2006) 'Making a European area of lifelong learning a reality? Some critical reflections on the European Union's lifelong learning policies', *Comparative Education*, 42: 49–62.

Dench, S. and Regan, J. (2000) *Learning in Later Life. Motivation and Impact*, Research Report 183, London: Department for Education and Employment.

Denton, F.T. and Spencer, B.G. (2008) *What Is Retirement? A Review and Assessment of Alternative Concepts and Measures*, SEDAP Research Paper No. 23, Hamilton, Ontario: McMaster University.

Department for Education and Employment (1998) *The Learning Age*. Cmd 3790, London: The Stationery Office.

Department for Education and Employment (1999) *Learning to Succeed.* Cmd 4932, London, The Stationery Office.

Department of Health (2001) *The National Service Framework for Older People*, London: Department of Health.

Department of Health (2004) 'Models of extra care and retirement communities', *Housing Learning & Improvement Network, Factsheet No. 4*, London: Department of Health.

Department for Innovation, Universities and Skills (2008) *Informal Adult Learning – Shaping the Way Ahead*, London: DIUS.

Dewar, B. (2005) 'Beyond tokenistic involvement of older people in research – a framework for future development and understanding', *International Journal of Older People Nursing* in association with *Journal of Clinical Nursing*, 14: 48–53.

Edwards, R. (1997) *Changing Places?* London: Routledge.

Edwards, R., Ranson, S. and Strain, M. (2002) 'Reflexivity: towards a theory of lifelong learning', *International Journal of Lifelong Education*, 21: 525–36.

Elderhostel, Inc. (2007) *Mental Stimulation and Lifelong Learning Activities in the 55+ Population.* Online. Available HTTP: http://www.elderhostel.com (accessed 17 September 2008).

Elmore, R. (1999) 'Education for older people: the moral dimension', *Education and Ageing*, 14: 9–20.

Engelbrecht, C. (2006) 'Educational gerontology: a professional imperative in education for the older Australian learner', *Australasian Journal on Ageing*, 25: 56–7.

Erikson, E. (1963; 2nd edn) *Childhood and Society*, New York, NY: Norton.

European Commission (2000) *Memorandum on Lifelong Learning.* Commission Staff Working Paper, Brussels: Commission of the European Communities.

European Commission (2002) 'Council Resolution of 27 June 2002 on Lifelong Learning', *Official Journal of the European Communities*, C163/1-3, Brussels.

European Commission (2006) *Adult Learning: It Is Never Too Late to Learn.* COM (2006) 614 final, Brussels.

European Commission (2007) *Action Plan on Adult Learning. It Is Always a Good Time to Learn.* COM (2007) 558 final, Brussels.

Field, J. (2000) 'Researching lifelong learning through focus groups', *Journal of Further and Higher Education*, 24: 323–35.

Findsen, B. (2005) *Learning Later*, Malabar: FLA: Krieger Publishing Company.

Ford. G. (2005) *Am I Still Needed? Guidance and Learning for Older Adults*, Derby: Centre for Guidance Studies, University of Derby.

Formosa, M. (2002) 'Critical geragogy: developing practical possibilities for critical educational gerontology', *Education and Ageing*, 13: 73–86.

Formosa, M. (2005) 'Feminism and critical educational gerontology: an agenda for good practice', *Ageing International*, 30: 396–411.

Formosa, M. (2007) 'A Bourdieusian interpretation of the University of the Third Age in Malta', *Journal of Maltese Education Research*, 4: 1–16.

Frankland, J. and Bloor, M. (1999) 'Some issues arising in the systematic analysis of focus group materials', in R.S. Barbour and J. Kitzinger (eds) *Developing Focus Group Research*, London: Sage Publications.

Friedan, B. (1993) *The Fountain of Age*, London: Jonathan Cape.

Gilleard, C. (1996) 'Consumption and identity in later life: towards a cultural gerontology, *Ageing and Society*, 16: 489–98.

Gilleard, C. and Higgs, P. (2005) *Contexts of Ageing*, Cambridge: Polity Press.

Glendenning, F. (1985) *Educational Gerontology: International Perspectives*, London: Croom Helm.

Glendenning, F. (1991) 'What is the future of educational gerontology?' *Ageing and Society*, 11: 209–16.

Glendenning, F. (1997) 'Why educational gerontology is not yet established as a field of study: some critical implications', *Education and Ageing*, 12: 82–91.

Glendenning, F. (2000a) 'The education for older adults "movement": an overview', in F. Glendenning (ed.) *Teaching and Learning in Later Life*, Aldershot: Ashgate.

Glendenning, F. (2000b) 'Educational and social gerontology: necessary relationships', in F. Glendenning (ed.) *Teaching and Learning in Later Life*, Aldershot: Ashgate.

Glendenning, F. and Battersby, D. (1990) 'Why we need educational gerontology and education for older adults: a statement of first principles', in F. Glendenning and K. Percy (eds) *Ageing, Education and Society. Readings in Educational Gerontology*, Keele: University of Keele.

Golding, B., Brown, M., Foley, A., Harvey, J. and Gleeson, L. (2007) *Men's Sheds in Australia. Learning through Community Contexts*, Adelaide: NCVER.

Gorard, S. and Selwyn, N. (2005) 'What makes a lifelong learner?' *Teachers College Record*, 107: 1193–216.

Gordon, L. and Shinagel, M. (2004) 'New goals for continuing higher education: the older learner', *Harvard Generations Policy Journal*, 1: 53–65.

Government Office for Science (GOScience) Foresight Mental Capital and Wellbeing Project. (2008) *Final Project Report – Executive Summary*, London: The Government Office for Science.

Green, A. (2002) 'The many faces of lifelong learning: recent education policy trends in Europe', *Journal of Educational Policy*, 17: 611–26.

Green, J. and Hart, L. (1999) 'The impact of context on data', in R.S. Barbour and J. Kitzinger (eds) *Developing Focus Group Research*, London: Sage Publications.

Hammond, C. (2004) 'Impact of lifelong learning upon emotional resilience, psychological and mental health: fieldwork evidence', *Oxford Review of Education*, 30: 551–68.

Harrison, R. (1988) *Learning Later. A Handbook for Developing Educational Opportunities with Older People*, Leicester: UDACE and the Open University.

Havighurst, R.J. (1963) 'Successful aging', in R.H. Williams, C. Tibbitts and W. Donahue (eds) *Processes of Aging 1*, New York, NY: Atherton.

Healy, T. and Slowey, M. (2006) 'Social exclusion and adult engagement in lifelong learning – some comparative implications for European states based on Ireland's Celtic Tiger experience', *Compare*, 36: 359–78.

Help the Aged (2008a) *Learning for Living: Helping to Prevent Social Exclusion among Older People*, London: Help the Aged.

Help the Aged (2008b) *Education for Older People. Help the Aged Policy Statement 2008*, London: Help the Aged.

Hiemstra, R. (1993) 'Older women's ways of learning: tapping the full potential', paper presented at the University of Nebraska at Omaha Conference on The Enduring Spirit: Women as They Age, Omaha, April. Online. Available HTTP: http://www-distance.syr.edu/unospeech.html (accessed 5 May 2005).

HM Government (2005) *Opportunity Age. Meeting the Challenges of Ageing in the 21st Century*, London: Department of Work and Pensions.

HM Government. (2008) *Opportunity Age: Volume Two. A Social Portrait of Ageing in the UK*, London: Department of Work and Pensions.

HM Treasury (2006) *Leitch Review of Skills. Prosperity for All in the Global Economy – World Class Skills. Final Report*, London: HM Treasury.

Hodkinson, P., Ford, G., Hodkinson, H. and Hawthorn, R. (2008) 'Retirement as a learning process', *Educational Gerontology*, 34: 167–84.

Jackson, S. (2006) 'Jam, Jerusalem and calendar girls. Lifelong learning and the Women's Institutes (WI)', *Studies in the Education of Adults*, 38: 74–90.

James, O. (2008) *Contented Dementia*, London: Vermilion.

Jamieson, A. (2002) 'Theory and practice in social gerontology', in A. Jamieson and C.R. Victor (eds) *Researching Ageing and Later Life*, Buckingham: Open University Press.

Jamieson, A., Miller, A. and Stafford, J. (1998) 'Education in a life course perspective', *Education and Ageing*, 13: 213–28.

Johnston, S. and Phillipson, C. (1983) *Older Learners*, London: Bedford Square Press/NCVO.

Jarvis, P. (1994) 'Learning, ageing and education in the risk society', *Education and Ageing*, 9: 6–20.

Katz, S. (1996) *Disciplining Old Age: The Formation of Gerontological Knowledge*, Charlottesville, VA: University Press of Virginia.

Katz, S. (2000) 'Busy bodies: activity, aging and the management of everyday life', *Journal of Aging Studies*, 14: 135–52.

Kelly, P. (1992) *Living and Learning: A Study of the Open University's Older Graduates*, Manchester: The Open University North West Region.

Kilpatrick, S., Field, J. and Falk, I. (2003) 'Social capital: an analytical tool for exploring lifelong learning and community development', *British Educational Research Journal*, 29: 417–33.

Kitwood, T. (1997) *Dementia Reconsidered: The Person Comes First*, Buckingham: Open University Press.

Kitzinger, J. and Barbour, R.S. (1999) 'Introduction: the challenge and promise of focus groups', in R.S. Barbour and J. Kitzinger (eds) *Developing Focus Group Research*, London: Sage Publications.

Knowles, M. and Associates (1984) *Andragogy in Action: Applying Modern Principles of Adult Learning*, San Francisco: Jossey-Bass.

Kotulak, R. (1997) *Inside the Brain: Revolutionary Discoveries of How the Mind Works*, Kansas City, KY: Andrews McNeel Publishing.

Kump, S. and Krašovec, S. (2007) 'Education: a possibility for empowering older adults', *International Journal of Lifelong Education*, 26: 635–49.

Lambeir, B. (2005) 'Education as liberation: the politics and techniques of lifelong learning', *Educational Philosophy and Theory*, 37: 349–55.

Larkin, M. (2007) 'University-based retirement communities on the rise', *The Journal on Active Ageing*, no number: 53–9.

Laslett, P. (1984) 'The education of the elderly in Britain', in E. Midwinter (ed.) *Mutual Aid Universities*, London: Croom Helm.

Laslett, P. (1989) *A Fresh Map of Life*, London: Weidenfeld and Nicolson.

Leamy, M. and Clough, R. (2006) *How Older People Become Researchers: Training, Guidance and Practice in Action*, York: Joseph Rowntree Foundation.

Leathwood, C. and Francis, B. (2006) 'Introduction: gendering lifelong learning', in C. Leathwood and B. Francis (eds) *Gender and Lifelong Learning. Critical Feminist Engagement*, Abingdon: Routledge.

Lemieux, A. and Sanchez Martinez, M. (2000) 'Gerontagogy beyond words: a reality', *Educational Gerontology*, 26: 479–98.

Luborsky, M.R. (1994) 'The identification of themes and patterns', in J.F. Gubrium and A. Sankar (eds) *Qualitative Methods in Aging Research*, Thousand Oaks, CA: Sage Publications.

McGivney, V. (1990) *Education's for Other People*, Leicester: NIACE.

McLafferty, I. (2004) 'Focus group interviews as a data collecting strategy', *Journal of Advanced Nursing*, 48: 187–94.

McNair, S. (2007) *Demography and Adult Learning. A Discussion Paper for the NIACE Committee of Inquiry*, Leicester: NIACE.

Maltby, T. (2008) 'Editorial', *Older and Bolder Newsletter*, 56: 1–2.

Mehrotra, C.M. (2003) 'In defense of offering educational programs for older adults', *Educational Gerontology*, 29: 645–55.

Merriam, S.B. and Mohamad, M. (2000) 'How cultural values shape learning in older adulthood: the case of Malaysia', *Adult Education Quarterly*, 51: 45–63.

Midwinter, E. (1984) *Mutual Aid Universities*, London: Croom Helm.

Neuberger, J. (2008) *Not Dead Yet. A Manifesto for Old Age*, London: HarperCollins.

Newman, S. and Hatton-Yeo, A. (2008) 'Intergenerational learning and the contribution of older people', *Ageing Horizons*, 8: 31–9.

NIACE (2007) *The Future for Lifelong Learning: A National Strategy*, Leicester: NIACE.

Nimrod, G. and Adoni, H. (2006) 'Leisure-styles and life satisfaction among recent retirees in Israel', *Ageing and Society*, 26: 607–30.

Oancea, A. (2008) 'The promise of lifelong learning', *Ageing Horizons*, 8: 1–3.

Office of the Deputy Prime Minister (2006) *A Sure Start to Later Life. Ending Inequalities for Older People*, London: Social Exclusion Unit Final Report.

Office for National Statistics (2007) *National Statistics Online. Ageing*. Online. Available HTTP: http://www.statistics.gov.uk/cci.nugget.asp?ID+949 (accessed 7 November 2007).

Office for National Statistics (2008) *Population Trends 13*. Online. Available HTTP: http://www.statistics.gov.uk/default.asp (accessed 1 October 2008).

O'Hagan, B. (1991) 'Empowerment: a fallacy?' *Community Education Network*, 11: 3–5.

Pépin, L. (2007) 'The history of EU cooperation in the field of education and training: how lifelong learning became a strategic objective', *European Journal of Education*, 42: 121–32.

Percy, K. (1990) 'The future of educational gerontology: a second statement of first principles', in F. Glendenning and K. Percy (eds) *Ageing, Education and Society. Readings in Educational Gerontology*, Keele: University of Keele.

Peterson. D. (1976) 'Educational gerontology: the state of the art', *Educational Gerontology*, 1: 61–73.

Phillipson, C. (1983) 'Education and the older learner: current developments and initiatives', in S. Johnston and C. Phillipson (eds) *Older Learners: The Challenge to Adult Education*, London: Bedford Square Press/NCVO.

Phillipson, C. (1998) *Reconstructing Old Age*, London: Sage Publications.

Poortman, A.-R. and Van Tilburg T.G. (2005) 'Past experiences and older adults' attitudes: a lifecourse perspective', *Ageing and Society*, 25: 19–39.

Powell Lawton, M. (1993) 'Meanings of activity', in J.R. Kelly (ed.) *Activity and Ageing*, Newbury Park, CA: Sage Publications.

Prokou, E. (2008) 'A comparative approach to lifelong learning policies in Europe: the case of the UK, Sweden and Greece', *European Journal of Education*, 43: 123–40.

Quine, S. (1998) 'Practical guidelines for organizing and running focus groups with older people', *Generations Review*, 8: 4–6.

Ritters, K. and Davis, H. (2008) *Access to Information and Services for Older People – the Joined-up Approach*, DWP Working Paper No. 53, London: Department for Works and Pensions.

Roberson, D.N. and Merriam, S.B. (2005) 'The self-directed learning process of older, rural adults', *Adult Education Quarterly*, 55: 269–87.

Russell, H. (2008) 'Later life: a time to learn', *Educational Gerontology*, 34: 206–24.

Salthouse T. (2006) 'Mental exercise and mental aging: evaluating the validity of the "Use It or Lose It" hypothesis', *Perspectives on Psychological Science*, 1: 68–87.

Sankar, A. and Gubrium, J.F. (1994) 'Introduction', in J.F. Gubrium and A. Sankar (eds) *Qualitiative Research Methods in Aging Research*, Thousand Oaks, CA: Sage Publications.

Schachter-Shalomi, Z. and Miller, R.S. (1997) *From Age-ing to Sage-ing*, New York, NY: Warner Books.

Schuetze, H. and Casey, C. (2006) 'Models and meanings of lifelong learning: progress and barriers on the road to a learning society', *Compare*, 36: 279–87.

Schuetze H.G. (2006) 'International concepts and agendas of lifelong learning', *Compare*, 36: 289–306.

Schuetze, H. (2007) 'Individual learning accounts and other models of financing lifelong learning', *International Journal of Lifelong Education*, 26: 5–23.

Schuller, T. and Bostyn, A.-M. (1992) *Learning, Education, Training and Information in the Third Age*, Carnegie Inquiry into the Third Age. Research Paper No. 3, Dunfermline: Carnegie UK Trust.

Scottish Executive (2007) *All Our Futures. Planning for a Scotland with an Ageing Population*, Edinburgh: Scottish Executive.

Sherron, R.H. and Lumsden, D.B. (1978; 3rd edn 1990) *An Introduction to Educational Gerontology*, Washington, DC: Hemisphere Publishing.

Slowey, M. (2008) 'Age is just a number', *Ageing Horizons*, 8: 22–30.

Smith, M.K. (1996; 2nd edn 1999) 'Andragogy', *The Encyclopaedia of Informal Education*. Online. Available HPPT: http://www.infed.org/lifelonglearning/6-andra.htm (accessed 2 October 2008).

Soulsby, J. (2000) *Mapping Learning Opportunities for Older People. Mapping Tool and Guidelines*, London: UK Secretariat for the International Year of Older People.

Soulsby, J. (2005) 'Older and Bolder: the NIACE campaign', in A. Tuckett and A. McAulay (eds) *Demography and Older Learners*, Leicester: NIACE.

Swindell, R. and Thompson, J. (1995) 'An international perspective on the University of the Third Age', *Educational Gerontology*, 21: 429–47.

Szinovacz, M. (1992) 'Social activities and retirement adaptation: gender and family variations', in M. Szinovacz, D.J. Ekerdt and B.H. Vinick (eds) *Families and Retirement*, Newby Park, CA: Sage Publications.

Tight, M. (1998) 'Education, education, education! The vision of lifelong learning in the Kennedy, Dearing and Fryer reports', *Oxford Review of Education*, 24: 473–85.

Tuschling, A. and Engemann, C. (2006) 'From education to lifelong learning. The emerging regime of learning in the European Union', *Educational Philosophy and Theory*, 38: 451–69.

UNESCO Commission on the World of Education Today and Tomorrow (1972) *Learning to Be*, Paris: UNESCO.

United Nations General Assembly (2006). Sixty-first session. Social development: follow-up to the International Year of Older People: Second World Assembly on Ageing, *Report of the Secretary-General*. Online. Available HTTP: http://www.un.org (accessed 8 October 2007).

United Nations Programme on Ageing (2006) *Madrid International Plan of Action on Ageing*. Online. Available HTTP: http://www.un.org (accessed 8 October 2007).

US Census Bureau International Database (2008) Online. Available HTTP: http://www.census.gov (accessed 6 January 2008).

Usher, R., Bryant, I. and Johnston, R. (1997) *Adult Education and the Postmodern Challenge*, London: Routledge.

Usher, R. and Edwards, R. (2007) *Lifelong Learning: Signs, Discourses, Practices*, Dordrecht: Springer.

Walker, A. (2002) 'A strategy for active ageing', *International Social Security Review*, 55: 121–39.

Walker, J. (1996) *Changing Concepts of Retirement*, Aldershot: Ashgate.

Wallace, J.B. (1994) 'Life stories', in J.F. Gubrium and A. Sankar (eds) *Qualitative Methods in Ageing Research*, Thousand Oaks, CA: Sage Publications.

Welsh Assembly Government (2003) *The Strategy for Older People in Wales*, Cardiff: Welsh Assembly Government.

Welsh Assembly Government (2008a) *The Strategy for Older People in Wales 2008–2013*, Cardiff: Welsh Assembly Government.

Welsh Assembly Government (2008b) *Building a Society for All Ages*. Draft Intergenerational Practice Strategy for Wales, Cardiff: Welsh Assembly Government.

Whitbourne, S. (2001) *Adult Development and Aging. Biopsychosocial Perspectives*, New York, NY: John Wiley & Sons.

Williamson, A. (2000) 'Gender issues in older adults' participation in learning: viewpoints and experiences of learners in the University of the Third Age', *Educational Gerontology*, 26: 49–66.

Wilson, V. (1997) 'Focus groups: a useful qualitative method for educational research?' *British Educational Research Journal*, 23: 209–22.

Withnall, A. (2000) 'Reflections on lifelong learning and the Third Age', in J. Field and M. Leicester (eds) *Lifelong Learning. Education Across the Lifespan*, London: Routledge Falmer.

Withnall, A. (2002) 'Three decades of educational gerontology: achievements and challenges', *Education and Ageing*, 17: 87–102.

Withnall, A. (2007a) *Ten Years Older – but Bolder. An Evaluation of the First Ten Years of the Older and Bolder Programme.* Unpublished report commissioned by NIACE.

Withnall, A. (2007b) 'The role of context in later life learning', in V. Bissland and B. McKechnie (eds) *Proceedings of the International Conference on Learning in Later Life, 9–11 May 2007*, Glasgow: University of Strathclyde, Senior Studies Institute.

Withnall, A. (2008) *Best Practice in the Delivery of Older People's Learning. A Review of the Literature.* Unpublished report commissioned by the Workers Educational Association Northern Ireland.

Withnall, A. and Percy, K. (1994) *Good Practice in the Education and Training of Older Adults*, Aldershot: Ashgate.

Withnall, A., McGivney, V. and Soulsby, J. (2004) *Older People Learning. Myths and Realities*, Leicester: NIACE.

Wolf, P. (2006) 'The role of meaning and emotion in learning', in S. Johnson and K. Taylor (eds) *The Neuroscience of Adult Learning. New Directions for Adult and Continuing Education*, 110, San Francisco: Jossey Bass.

World Health Organization (2002) *Active Ageing. A Policy Framework*, Geneva: WHO.

Index